"WHEN WE DON'T HAVE THE WORDS
CHOCOLATE CAN SPEAK VOLUMES."

JOAN BAUER

I ♥ CHOCOLATE

I LOVE THERMOMIX

MOUTHWATERING AND DELICIOUS CHOCOLATE RECIPES FROM MASTERS OF THE ART OF CHOCOLATE

BEVERLEY DUNKLEY ♥ DIRK SCHONKEREN ♥ IAIN BURNETT ♥ JOHN HUBER

JOHN SLATTERY ♥ MARK TILLING ♥ RUTH HINKS ♥ THIERRY DUMOUCHEL

I ♥ CHOCOLATE I ♥ THERMOMIX

First published in 2013 by Chef Books and Cook With Janie Ltd.

Chef Books
Network House, 28 Ballmoor, Celtic Court
Buckingham MK18 1RQ, UK
www.chefmagazine.co.uk

© Chef Books/Cook With Janie Ltd.

Cook With Janie Ltd.
Pinehill, Sunning Avenue
Sunningdale, Berkshire SL5 9PW, UK
www.cookwithjanie.com

ISBN 978-1-908202-15-4

Printed by M.P. Printing in China

Publisher: Peter Marshall
Author: Janie Turner
Editors: Helen Homes, Shirley Marshall
Recipe testing: Janie Turner, Caroline Snook
Photography: Ben Pollard, Caroline Snook, Chris Orange
Myburgh du Plessis, Peter Marshall
Designer: Philip Donnelly

INTRODUCTION

With its enticing aroma, its brilliant sheen, its sensuous melt, there is nothing like it. Chocolate guarantees a moment of enchantment. There is a world of seduction in a delicate mousse, a melting cookie, a classic gateau, a dark truffle, and a spicy hot chocolate, all of them featured in the following pages. In 76 recipes, by 8 top chocolatiers, *I Love Chocolate, I Love Thermomix* contains a heavenly selection of creations for every occasion.

The great surprise about the chocolate we enjoy today is that it was ever invented. It comes from the bean inside the cocoa pod, a fruit that grows directly on the trunk of the tree. Yet the bean needs to go through many stages of processing before it becomes the bar or callet which forms the basis of all the recipes here. It has taken centuries of development to learn how to release the several hundred flavours in cocoa and develop the silky feel. Fermenting and roasting, winnowing and conching are all essential processes in the journey from the bean to the bar, and each has to be managed correctly to ensure a perfect finish.

To the Olmecs, the Maya and the Aztecs in Central America, chocolate was a divine gift which they served as a drink (though admittedly it would have been rather thin and unpleasant to our taste). A cocoa drink is how it was first enjoyed when it was brought to Europe. Gradually chefs started to experiment and learned to add the sweet spices, the sugar and the cream or butter that we have come to expect in our chocolate.

Of course, there's no one type of chocolate. The cook and chef today can vary the recipe depending on the chocolate chosen. Cocoa is grown around the world – from Central America to Africa, to Indonesia and Vietnam – and in every origin the flavours are subtly different. Sometimes a blend will be perfect for the recipe, for others a 'single origin chocolate' works best. The choice is yours and the variety is enormous. The only way to find the right one is to start experimenting. Cocoa percentages are usually mentioned for milk and dark chocolates used in this book, so use these as a guideline to your choices. Working with your Thermomix, you will find creating the recipes in *I Love Chocolate, I Love Thermomix* a really enjoyable process. Preparation times are halved; so too is clearing up and cleaning. With all the weighing, mixing, whisking, melting and cooking done in one bowl, creating chocolate delicacies becomes a pleasure. There are simple classics for family weekends, and impressive delights to wow diners.

Before you start cooking, read the sections on tempering (pre-crystallising) chocolate and making ganaches in your Thermomix (pages 16-22). Using your Thermomix means they could not be simpler or more straightforward. Master these techniques to guarantee a professional finish. All the recipes here have been contributed by Master Chocolatiers who are award-winning chefs and experienced professionals. Their recipes are tried and tested and are guaranteed to bring you pleasure and praise, time and again.

BEVERLEY DUNKLEY

BEVERLEY DUNKLEY IS HEAD OF THE UK CHOCOLATE ACADEMY AT BARRY CALLEBAUT IN BANBURY, OXFORDSHIRE, AND TEACHES CHOCOLATIERS AT ALL LEVELS FROM THE HOME HOBBY CHOCOLATE LOVER TO THE FINEST CHOCOLATE SCULPTORS AND PASTRY CHEFS.

Beverley has a real passion for patisserie and chocolate work.

In her early career she moved to Switzerland to work in the Sugar School of world-renowned pastry chef Ewald Notter, then she worked with Relais Desserts in Luxembourg where first-hand experience was gained in the production of French and German patisserie. She later became a lecturer in Patisserie at Morecambe College of Further Education teaching 16-19 year olds Baking skills and the art of Patisserie. She joined Barry Callebaut in 1995 and was initially responsible for the management of direct chocolate and distributor accounts in the South of England.

Beverley has been in demand as a judge at the SBST Bakery Student Awards, Hotelympia, the UK Chocolate Masters, and has helped organise the Junior UK Chocolate Masters.

Beverley is committed to helping people learn new chocolate skills and develop their careers and she loves to promote a desire to work with chocolate. She regularly runs Thermomix Chocolate Masterclasses with Janie Turner. "At the Academy, we use our Thermomix machines in a wide range of applications from making chocolate ganaches to producing pastry creams. We moved away from more time-consuming conventional ways of working with a stove, whisk, pots and pans around four or five years ago. Thermomix is easy to use, labour saving and reliable and saves us a huge amount of time and effort when preparing for our courses, demonstrations and customer presentations."

In her own words, "Chocolate is fun to eat and work with and I hope you enjoy making and eating the recipes I have prepared for you in this book."

www.chocolate-academy.com

DIRK SCHONKEREN

DIRK SCHONKEREN IS A CHEF AND MASTER CHOCOLATIER
WITH 40 YEARS EXPERIENCE. AS A YOUNG BOY HE
WORKED IN LOCAL RESTAURANTS AND IN HIS MOTHER'S
DELICATESSEN AND GRADUATED FROM THE PRESTIGIOUS
PIVA COLLEGE IN ANTWERP, BELGIUM. DIRK HELD
NUMEROUS POSITIONS AS CHEF DE PARTIE AND AS A
PASTRY CHEF IN RESTAURANTS AND HOTELS IN ANTWERP
AND BRUSSELS.

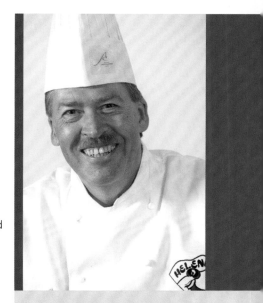

With his Irish wife Elaine O'Mahony, he moved to Ireland to take up
the position of Culinary Arts lecturer in Rockwell College.

Dirk also worked as executive head chef in some of Ireland's top
hotels and in 1983 won the National Dairy Council "Irish Cheese Board and
Cheese Recipe" competition.

Together with his wife Elaine he set up an artisan chocolaterie and
named it Helena Chocolates, supplying restaurants, hotels and speciality
shops with beautiful chocolate creations. They opened their first chocolate
shop in Castlebar, Co. Mayo in 1988 and a second shop in Galway in 1992.

Dirk was a finalist in the UK Chocolate Masters in 2006, and in 2007
Helena Chocolates moved to larger premises and opened a chocolate shop
with a restaurant and dessert lounge.

In 2009 Dirk was invited to join the Callebaut Ambassador's Club as
their first Irish ambassador.

As well as managing a busy chocolate shop and restaurant, Dirk
still finds the time for making exquisite chocolate sculptures, creating
gastronomic dishes with chocolate as well as continuing to teach the arts
of chocolate and pastry.

www.dumouchel.co.uk

IAIN BURNETT

IAIN BURNETT HIGHLAND CHOCOLATIER

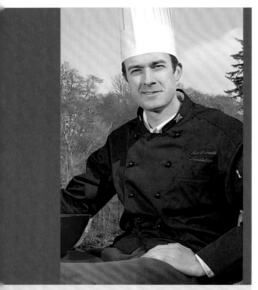

WORLD CLASS CHOCOLATIER IAIN BURNETT HIGHLAND CHOCOLATIER HAS BECOME INTERNATIONALLY RECOGNISED AS A MASTER TRUFFLE SPECIALIST. HIS OUTSTANDING CHOCOLATES HAVE GARNERED THE CHOCOLATE WORLD'S HIGHEST ACCOLADES: SWEEPING GOLD, SILVER AND BRONZE FROM THE ACADEMY OF CHOCOLATE; TRIPLE GOLD STARS IN THE NATIONAL GREAT TASTE AWARDS; AND TWICE EXCELLENCE AWARDS FROM SCOTLAND FOOD AND DRINK.

From his bespoke chocolate kitchen near Pitlochry in Highland Perthshire, Iain Burnett Highland Chocolatier creates chocolates of an unparalleled quality for a selection of high profile gourmet chefs and retailers. Clients include 5 star hotels, Michelin star restaurants and prestigious venues throughout the world. Iain's website expresses his passion, which is also clearly apparent to those who have visited his award-winning tourist attraction The Scottish Chocolate Centre.

Iain learned his initial culinary skills from his father who trained him from a young age to select from amongst the best of Scottish ingredients and exotic spices to create new flavours and textures. His passion for chocolate began in Japan upon discovering a Maître Chocolatier there who had created an exceptional truffle using only natural ingredients.

Iain's training under Master Chocolatiers of the Belgian, Swiss and French schools led to the creation of his own renowned collection of Velvet Truffles™ and Spiced Pralines. His Velvet Truffles™ are testimony to the virtues of patience and excellence plus high quality single-origin cocoa and fresh local Scottish cream. Iain and his team's pièce de résistance is the Cocoa Dusted Velvet Truffle™ – exquisite and unique in the breadth of its flavour profile and silky texture. It is served "naked", rather than enrobed in a hard chocolate shell, as a petit four with a truffle fork.

Iain dedicated more than 3 years to the refinement of his signature Velvet Truffle™ method and in the process developed what is required to be a genuine artisan chocolatier.

www.HighlandChocolatier.com

6

JOHN HUBER

WIDELY KNOWN AS THE KING OF PASTRY AND ONE OF THE UK'S MOST INFLUENTIAL PASTRY CHEFS, THE LATE JOHN HUBER WAS BORN IN SWITZERLAND BUT REGARDED ENGLAND AS HIS ADOPTED COUNTRY. HIS CONTRIBUTION TO FINE PASTRY WORK IN THE UK WAS PART OF A LENGTHY AND DISTINGUISHED CAREER STARTING IN 1967 WHEN HE JOINED SLOUGH COLLEGE OF HIGHER EDUCATION AS A LECTURER.

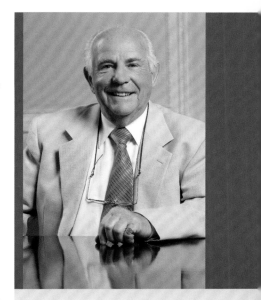

The department he joined was then known as the department of domestic science, art, hairdressing, pottery and catering, with catering being regarded as the poor relation.

Undeterred, Huber put together the first two-year day-release pastry course which culminated in a six hour practical examination, by using as a role model, the Swiss National Diploma for pâtissiers, confisseurs and glaciers, a diploma for which he himself had studied. Backed by the City & Guilds, the first students joined the course in 1972 and this was to form the basis of two advanced pastry courses which were to remain the mainstay of pastry education in the UK. He then spent over 30 years at Thames Valley University, where he transformed forever the way pastry was taught in the UK. His achievements were recognised in 1995 when he was invested as a Professor of Pastry, becoming the first pastry chef to be awarded the honour in the UK.

As well as being a pioneer in pastry education, John was equally well known in the industry for his enormous skill, enthusiasm and tireless energy. His teaching saw many of his students gain key roles in some of the best hotels and restaurants.

Huber recognised the need to continuously learn and was as enthusiastic as any of the students he taught in expanding his skills. He would regularly use a summer vacation to go to the continent to study saying "You are never too old to learn; I was in my 50's and was the oldest stagière they'd ever had!"

John's legacy to pastry education and the development of pastry in this country lives on and we hope that you enjoy preparing and eating his chocolate recipes included in this book.

JOHN SLATTERY

Having worked in baking and confectionery all his life, and being part of the family business for over 40 years, spending every day with his favourite ingredient was a natural move for John. After training at college, John attended courses in the chocolate capitals of the world; Switzerland, Belgium and Austria among others, gaining both skills and experience. His passion for chocolate is clear, as John is a member of the British Confectioners Association, The National Association of Master Bakers and the International Richemont Club – a centre for master bakers and confectioners.

Now John shares his love of chocolate with others, in the form of Slattery Pâtissier & Chocolatier Ltd, a three storey chocolate shop based on Bury New Road in Whitefield, Manchester. Affectionately known as 'That wicked shop', this unique store specialises in celebration cakes and chocolate treats, and prides itself on being able to create anything in chocolate! Of course, hand-made chocolates and chocolate gifts are also available, plus a dining room above, offering breakfast, lunch and afternoon tea.

John also offers a variety of courses in chocolate, cake decorating and other confectionery on the third floor of the shop, otherwise known as The School of Excellence. It is here that he and his staff meet many chocolate lovers who wish to advance their skills.

John has written two books, *'Chocolate Unwrapped'* and *'John Slattery's Creative Chocolate'* and he says with a smile, "After all, the art of chocolate doesn't need to be just for experts."

Unwrap your chocolate potential with John's inspirational and delicious recipes and give in to your own love of chocolate with *'I Love Chocolate I Love Thermomix'*!

JOHN SLATTERY HAS ALWAYS BEEN A LITTLE IN LOVE WITH CHOCOLATE – EATING IT, COOKING WITH IT, CREATING WITH IT – FOR JOHN, CHOCOLATE CAN BE USED TO CREATE A MILLION POSSIBILITIES.

w w w . s l a t t e r y . c o . u k

8

MARK TILLING

MARK TILLING HAS BEEN WORKING FOR OVER 20 YEARS IN THE PATISSERIE AND CHOCOLATE WORLD FOR WHICH HE HAS A GREAT PASSION. HE STARTED WORKING IN A HOTEL AT WEEKENDS BEFORE HE LEFT SCHOOL AND HAS WORKED IN MANY DIFFERENT HOTELS AND RESTAURANTS AROUND THE UK INCLUDING THE LANESBOROUGH ON HYDE PARK, LAINSTON HOUSE HOTEL IN WINCHESTER, HOTEL DU VIN WINCHESTER AND BRISTOL AND LE PAVE D'AUGE IN NORMANDY, FRANCE, WHICH BOASTS A MICHELIN STAR.

Mark has received many awards for his chocolate and patisserie work over the years. He has earned many gold and silver medals in desserts and petits fours as well as double gold in chocolate showpieces. His biggest achievement was twice winning the UK Chocolate Masters over a four year period from 2006-2010. He then represented the UK in the finals of the World Chocolate Masters in 2007 and 2009 coming 12th in 2007 and 7th in 2009. Coming 7th was the highest-ever UK placing and a great honour.

Now he teaches at Squires Kitchen International School in Farnham, Surrey, providing courses in chocolate and patisserie including five day chocolate schools, macaroon days and French patisserie classes. Mark says, "It's a great pleasure teaching and passing on my knowledge to everyone who comes to Squires."

Mark has written two books for Squires Kitchen *'Working with Chocolate'* and *'Making Macaroons'* and will soon be publishing a third book on chocolate wedding cakes and all sweet things.

Mark has used Thermomix for his competition work and teaching for many years and comments, " Thermomix, the best machine on the market – what can it not do! I couldn't have been without it at the World Chocolate Masters 2009. Thermomix takes competition work to the next level, I love it!"

w w w . s q u i r e s - s c h o o l . c o . u k

9

RUTH HINKS

AS THE CURRENT HOLDER OF THE PRESTIGIOUS 'UK CHOCOLATE MASTER' TITLE, RUTH HAS WORKED AS A PROFESSIONAL CHOCOLATIER AND PASTRY CHEF FOR OVER TWO DECADES. HER PASSION FOR COMPETITION AND DESIRE TO WORK WITH THE VERY BEST IN THE INDUSTRY HAS BROUGHT HER WIDESPREAD ACCLAIM AND RECOGNITION. PRIOR TO BECOMING THE UK CHOCOLATE MASTER, RUTH WAS ALSO NAMED UK CONFECTIONER OF THE YEAR 2011, AUSTRALIAN PASTRY CHEF OF THE YEAR AND WON GOLD AND SILVER MEDALS AT THE CULINARY OLYMPICS IN 2000 AND 2004.

Prior to launching Cocoa Black, Ruth held Head Pastry Chef positions with numerous 5-star hotels, most recently the Sheraton Grand Hotel in Edinburgh. She trained at the Cocoa Barry Chocolate School in Paris and the Carma Chocolate Academy in Switzerland. Ruth's love for chocolate started aged 14 when as a schoolgirl she would make and sell handmade Easter eggs to raise pocket money.

As a founder and director of the chocolate manufacturer Cocoa Black, Ruth is now spending as much time in the boardroom and at international demonstrations as she does in her production kitchen. With the launch of the Cocoa Black Chocolate & Pastry School in Peebles, near Edinburgh, Ruth now creates and delivers chocolate and pastry training for professional and domestic cooks. The Cocoa Black shop and café has grown rapidly, as has interest in the company's website which is now receiving orders from all over the world.

www.cocoablack.com

THIERRY DUMOUCHEL

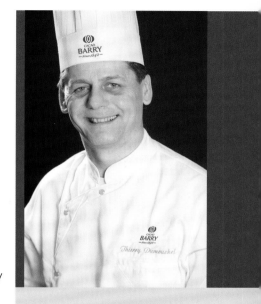

BORN AND RAISED IN RURAL NORMANDY, FROM A VERY YOUNG AGE THIERRY LEARNED TO APPRECIATE THE VALUE OF FRESH, QUALITY FOOD. AS PART OF A FARMING FAMILY, HE TOOK PART IN THE GROWING AND REARING OF THE FOOD THEY ATE AND IS A GREAT BELIEVER IN THE SAYING 'YOU ARE WHAT YOU EAT!' THIERRY HAS ALWAYS BEEN AGAINST THE ADDITION OF ANY ARTIFICIAL CHEMICALS AND PRESERVATIVES TO THE FOOD WE CONSUME. IT IS THIS PHILOSOPHY THAT INSPIRES HIM TO CREATE THE BREADS, CAKES AND PASTRIES WHICH MAKES DUMOUCHEL SO SPECIAL.

Thierry Dumouchel trained at the renowned food college in Rouen, France, and worked in Paris, London, Sydney and Tokyo before opening his patisserie in 1998 in Yorkshire. As a master of his craft and as UK ambassador for Barry Callebaut and the world renowned Cointreau, Thierry is often called upon to do demonstrations. He also works as a consultant offering advice and guidance to individuals and businesses around the UK and has been technical director and senior lecturer for the world famous Le Cordon Bleu Organisation.

In 2012, Dumouchel patisserie was extremely proud to have won The Baking Industry "Craft Business Award". The same year also saw the launch of Thierry's online artisan bread. The freshly baked bread is delivered by courier, lightly baked, bagged and ready to freeze. Simply defrost, finish in the oven and enjoy!

"Baking and chocolate are things to be savoured and definitely not rushed. All our breads, cakes and chocolate creations are made very naturally. We simply use good ingredients, and we don't add chemicals, ever! This produces flavour and quality. We simply refuse to compromise." Thierry's recipes reflect this approach and we hope you enjoy them!

www.dumouchel.co.uk

"MAN CANNOT LIVE ON CHOCOLATE ALONE; BUT WOMAN SURE CAN."

ANON

CONTENTS

UNDERSTANDING TEMPERING

CHOCOLATE IS ONE OF THE MOST WONDERFUL COMMODITIES TO WORK WITH. THE WAY IT LOOKS, FEELS AND OF COURSE TASTES, IS EXQUISITE. HOWEVER IT IS IMPORTANT TO HAVE A KNOWLEDGE AND UNDERSTANDING OF ITS COMPLEXITIES IF YOU ARE TO HAVE CONSISTENTLY SUCCESSFUL RESULTS WHEN WORKING WITH CHOCOLATE. CHOCOLATE'S ONLY LIMITS ARE YOUR OWN IMAGINATION!

Tempering chocolate is an important process for a number of reasons, including the influence it has on the look and taste of the finished product. It determines the amount and quality of pre-crystallising achieved with the cocoa butter present in the chocolate. Pre-crystallising is essential to create the right amount of stable cocoa butter crystals so your chocolate sets perfectly.

Cocoa butter is the fat of the cocoa bean, and it is the presence of cocoa butter that:

☺ **Creates chocolate with a good gloss/shine**
☺ **Allows chocolate to release easily from moulds as it contracts**
☺ **Has a sensational mouth feel, melting in the mouth**
☺ **Gives chocolate a hardness so that it snaps when broken**

However it is the same cocoa butter that can:

☹ **Give chocolate white streaks over its surface (fat bloom)**
☹ **Cause it to melt very quickly when touched**
☹ **Make it feel grainy on the tongue (sugar bloom)**
☹ **Cause it to bend and break without its characteristic snap**

SO HOW IS THIS POSSIBLE?

The reasons for chocolate behaving so very differently is because cocoa butter is polymorphic, which means it can change depending on its environment and how it is handled.

Chocolatiers now know that it's not just the temperature of the chocolate that matters but also the crystal formation at the time of preparation.

Cocoa butter is known to contain six different crystals and these will be present in your chocolate in different amounts depending on the varying amounts of time, temperature and movement given to the chocolate. Unfortunately not all of these six crystals have a stable structure and most of them don't lock together when set. It is only when the stable crystals are present in the right quantities that you will be able to achieve all the desirable qualities of chocolate.

We also now know that if chocolate does not receive sufficient movement when being melted, insufficient stable crystals will develop to allow the good characteristics of cocoa butter to emerge. Since Thermomix stirs as it melts, it is perfect to use as your tool of choice for tempering as well as for making the delicious chocolate recipes in *'I Love Chocolate I Love Thermomix'*.

EQUIPMENT:
Thermomix TM31
Thermomix spatula

MELTING CHOCOLATE

Good quality chocolate contains cocoa butter which melts at a temperature just below our own body temperature. This temperature similarity is why chocolate provides such a luxurious sensation when we eat it.

It is important not to overheat chocolate. Because chocolate can burn easily, we need to be aware of the best temperature range in which to work with it. Thermomix has accurate temperature settings for 37°C and 50°C, both of which are in this range, and you will see in the next section (pre-crystallising chocolate) how to use these temperature settings to melt and temper chocolate.

MILK AND WHITE CHOCOLATE:
The methods in the next section for pre-crystallising chocolate are the same for white, milk and dark varieties. However, due to the additional milk and sugar content of milk and white chocolate, they will melt more quickly than dark chocolates, and their tempered temperatures are slightly lower.

PRE-CRYSTALLISING CHOCOLATE

EQUIPMENT:
Thermomix TM31
Thermomix spatula
Digital temperature probe

PRE-CRYSTALLISING TIPS:
CHOCOLATE CAN BE PRE-CRYSTALLISED IN MANY WAYS. HERE ARE TWO THERMOMIX METHODS (WITH EXAMPLES) TO MELT CHOCOLATE WITH JUST THE RIGHT AMOUNTS OF HEAT, MOVEMENT AND TIME IN ORDER TO TAKE IT TO THE CORRECT TEMPERATURE FOR CREATING STABLE COCOA BUTTER CRYSTALS.

THE IDEAL ROOM ENVIRONMENT FOR WORKING WITH CHOCOLATE IS 19-21°C WITH DE-HUMIDIFIERS RUNNING TO KEEP THE ATMOSPHERE DRY. AS MOST HOME KITCHENS DON'T HAVE A DE-HUMIDIFIER AND THE ROOM TEMPERATURE MAY VARY FROM ONE DAY TO ANOTHER, YOU MAY FIND YOU HAVE TO ADAPT THE FOLLOWING METHODS SLIGHTLY TO YOUR OWN ENVIRONMENT. TIMINGS FOR TEMPERING AND FOR SETTING CHOCOLATE WILL BE DIFFERENT IN DIFFERENT ENVIRONMENTS AND WILL ALSO DEPEND ON THE SIZE AND DENSITY OF THE CHOCOLATE ITEM BEING SET.

PRE-CRYSTALLISING CHOCOLATE REQUIRES:

- ☺ **TIME**
- ☺ **TEMPERATURE**
- ☺ **MOVEMENT**
- ☺ **TESTING**

TARGET TEMPERATURES FOR TEMPERING:

DARK CHOCOLATE	**32-34°C**
MILK CHOCOLATE	**31-32°C**
WHITE CHOCOLATE	**29-30°C**

As with any new skill, pre-crystallising needs practice, and the recipes in this book will give you opportunities to learn and improve while enjoying delicious chocolate treats!

SEEDING METHOD:

Fully melt about 75% of the desired weight of tempered chocolate, then add in about 25% of desired weight (as pre-crystallised callets or small pieces) then stir without added heat until all the chocolate is melted and smooth – the addition of the extra callets "seeds in" some stable cocoa butter crystals and drops the melted chocolate temperature down to the tempered range. Here is an example:

450G CALLEBAUT 811 NV DARK CHOCOLATE 54%, CALLETS OR SMALL PIECES

1. Melt 7 minutes/50°C/Speed 1 or 2, pausing once to scrape down the sides of the TM bowl with the spatula.
2. Remove the TM lid and check the temperature of the melted chocolate with a digital temperature probe:
   - if it reads over 40°C add 150g chocolate
   - if it reads 39°C add 85g chocolate
   - if it reads 38°C add 70g chocolate
3. Stir 2 minutes/Speed 2/TM Measuring Cup OFF without heat until all the callets are melted and the chocolate is completely smooth.
4. Remove the TM lid and check the temperature with the probe (wiped clean first). You are aiming for 32-34°C.
5. Test chocolate on a piece of paper (see next page for method).

PARTIAL MELTING METHOD:

Melt with gentle heat until about 60% of the chocolate is melted, then stir without heat to melt remaining callets completely and to reach tempered temperature range. Here is an example:

500G CALLEBAUT 811 NV DARK CHOCOLATE 54%, SMALL PIECES OR CALLETS

1. Melt 4 minutes/37°C/Speed 1, pausing once to scrape down the sides of the TM bowl.
2. Remove the TM lid and check temperature:
   - If the chocolate is 32-33°C and fully melted, test (see step 4).
   - If the chocolate is 34-36°C with a few unmelted callets still present, stir without heat 3 minutes/Speed 2 then test (see step 4).
   - If the chocolate is 32°C or less, with a few unmelted callets still present, heat again 20 seconds/37°C/Speed 1 then stir without heat until all callets are melted; remove TM lid and check that the temperature is 32-34°C. Repeat if necessary until correct temperature is reached. Test (see step 3).
   - If the chocolate is above 34°C add a few callets to melt slowly within the chocolate to take the temperature to 32-34°C. Test (see step 3).
3. Test chocolate on a piece of paper (see next page for method).

TESTING THE CHOCOLATE

EQUIPMENT:
Thermomix TM31
Small pieces of greaseproof
    paper
Clock or timer

TESTING YOUR CHOCOLATE IS THE MOST IMPORTANT THING YOU CAN DO WHEN DETERMINING IF CHOCOLATE IS PRE-CRYSTALLISED AND READY TO USE. THIS WILL TELL YOU, BEFORE YOU START USING THE CHOCOLATE, HOW YOUR PRODUCTS WILL SET.

THE 3 STAGES OF SETTING CHOCOLATE:
1. **MELTED:** chocolate is fluid
2. **TOUCH DRY:** Chocolate becomes touch dry when left to set
3. **COMPLETELY DRY:** Chocolate contracts and is completely set throughout

Take a small rectangle of greaseproof paper and dip it into the chocolate. Place it (chocolate side up) on a clean surface and leave to set.

If it sets in 2 minutes in an environment of 19-21°C and has a shine, the chocolate has enough stable crystals and is ready to use.

However, if the chocolate is still fluid after 2 minutes, you have some stable crystals but not enough to give the chocolate a good gloss and snap when eaten. To correct this, stir at Speed 2 for a minute or two (depending on the volume of chocolate) to create some extra crystals with or without adding some more callets to the liquid chocolate. Either way will increase the amount of crystals. Repeat the test.

If it sets in 2 minutes in an environment of 19-21°C but is streaky, stir 3 minutes/Speed 2 without the TM Measuring Cup and test again. It should now set with a shine.

If however the chocolate sets in under 2 minutes and/or sets with bubbles under the surface, this means that you have good stable crystals, but too many of them. Having too many might sound like a good thing but it will make the chocolate thick and very hard to work with. In this case, all that is required is a little heat to reduce the amount of crystals so melt again 20 seconds/37°C/Speed 2, then repeat the test.

It's also worth remembering that melted or tempered chocolate left in your TM bowl will gradually cool and thicken. This is easily solved by warming and stirring little and often to keep the chocolate at its optimum fluidity for easy working – do this before it gets too thick.

The Sacher Torte recipe in this book describes practical tips for achieving a glossy ganache, and you can also use them to keep your chocolate melted and tempered – see p48.

NOTE:
Always stop your Thermomix and remove the TM lid before using your temperature probe.

Setting with bubbles – too many crystals

Setting with streaks – too warm

STORING CHOCOLATE

The ideal storage temperature for chocolate items is 11-12°C in a de-humidified fridge.

If you have a wine fridge that is set at 12°C, it would make an ideal storage place for your chocolate items too.

If you are going to store them in a normal kitchen fridge, you would need to put them into a fridge that is maximum 10°C lower than your room temperature as 10°C is the largest change in temperature that chocolate can handle at a time. However, most domestic fridges are cooler than this and if you put freshly made chocolate items straight into a 2-5°C fridge, you will shock the chocolate by cooling it too quickly. This may cause it to develop a fat bloom or sugar bloom.

Beverley Dunkley therefore suggests a two-stage process. First cool your chocolate items down to 10°C above your fridge temperature, either in a colder/air-conditioned room, in a north-facing pantry, or with a fan. Once they are within 10°C of your fridge temperature, you may store them in your fridge if desired.

When you remove your chocolate items from the fridge, bring them to room temperature slowly to avoid attracting condensation which may spoil their looks.

CHOCOLATE IS VERY SENSITIVE TO ABSORBING AROMAS, THEREFORE:

- Always keep your bags and packs of chocolate well wrapped up and store them in a cool place away from strong smelling items.
- After thoroughly washing and drying your TM bowl, give the lid seal a chance to air to keep it fragrance free.

Ruth Hinks World Chocolate Masters showpiece

COLD EMULSION METHOD FOR SCULPTURE CHOCOLATE

- 200g chocolate, small pieces or callets
- Grate 5 seconds/Speed 10.

WHITE CHOCOLATE, E.G. CALLEBAUT 823NV
Mix 1 minute/Speed 4½ – JUST until a smooth paste is created – this is easy to work with to create sculptured items. If it becomes too stiff to work with, simply return to the TM bowl and mix at Speed 4½ until it becomes a workable smooth paste again.

DARK CHOCOLATE 54%, E.G. CALLEBAUT 811NV
Mix 1½ minutes/Speed 4½ – scrape down TM bowl – allow to harden – mix again JUST until a smooth paste is created – this is easy to work with to create sculptured items. If it becomes too stiff to work with, simply return to the TM bowl and mix at Speed 4½ until it becomes a workable smooth paste again.

GANACHES

GANACHE IS A TERM DESCRIBING CHOCOLATE THAT IS MELTED WITH OTHER LIQUIDS, MOST OFTEN CREAM, AND TO WHICH EXTRA FLAVOURS MAY BE ADDED, FOR EXAMPLE A LIQUEUR OR A FRUIT PUREE. THE OTHER LIQUIDS MAY ALSO BE INFUSED WITH FLAVOUR FROM HERBS OR SPICES, AS IN THE MILK CHOCOLATE MINT BAR RECIPE ON P84.

GANACHES CAN BE USED IN THE FOLLOWING WAYS:

- Poured while still in their liquid state over a cake as a topping
- Cooled to 27-30°C then piped into chocolate shells (i.e. the ganache is the centre of hand-made chocolates)
- Left to fully set at room temperature and
- Rolled into balls or cut into shapes to serve as chocolate truffles or
- Whisked to aerate so it can be used to fill or decorate a cake

THE ADVANTAGES OF MAKING AND CREATING GANACHES IN YOUR THERMOMIX ARE MANY:

- One bowl
- Built-in weighing scales
- Built-in accurate temperature control
- Stirring at up to Speed 2 avoids incorporating air
- Less waste between steps
- Cleaner working area
- Ganaches can be homogenised (improves stability of the ganache and extends shelf life)
- Excellent for recipe development
- Much less washing up!

All these recipes have been tested with room-temperature eggs and chocolate, i.e. at room temperature of 21C.

If your ingredients or room temperature are different, you may find that the timings in these recipes need to be adjusted accordingly.

i ♥ CHOCOLATE
BUYING CHOCOLATE

All the recipes in this book have been tested with Callebaut chocolate containing only cocoa butter i.e. no vegetable oils or fats. We recommend using the Callebaut brand whenever possible in order to get excellent results. To make it easy for you to buy Callebaut chocolate, our website www.ilovechoc.net links to an online shop where you can purchase this high quality chocolate in small and large quantities.

These are the Callebaut chocolates we have used in our recipes:

Callebaut 70-30-38 dark chocolate 70%	300g	1kg	5kg
Callebaut 811 NV dark chocolate 54%	300g	1kg	5kg
Callebaut 823 NV milk chocolate 33%	300g	1kg	5kg
Callebaut W2 NV white chocolate	300g	1kg	5kg
Callebaut caramel flavoured chocolate	300g		

You may also like to try using single origin chocolate.

Callebaut Origin chocolates, also available via www.ilovechoc.net, include the following and others may be available on request:

Java milk chocolate 32%
Ecuador dark chocolate 70%
Grenade dark chocolate 60%
Saothome dark chocolate 70%
Madagascar dark chocolate 67%

www.ilovechoc.net

The author, Janie Turner, teaching a Thermomix Chocolate Masterclass at the Barry Callebaut Chocolate Academy
www.cookwithjanie.com

23

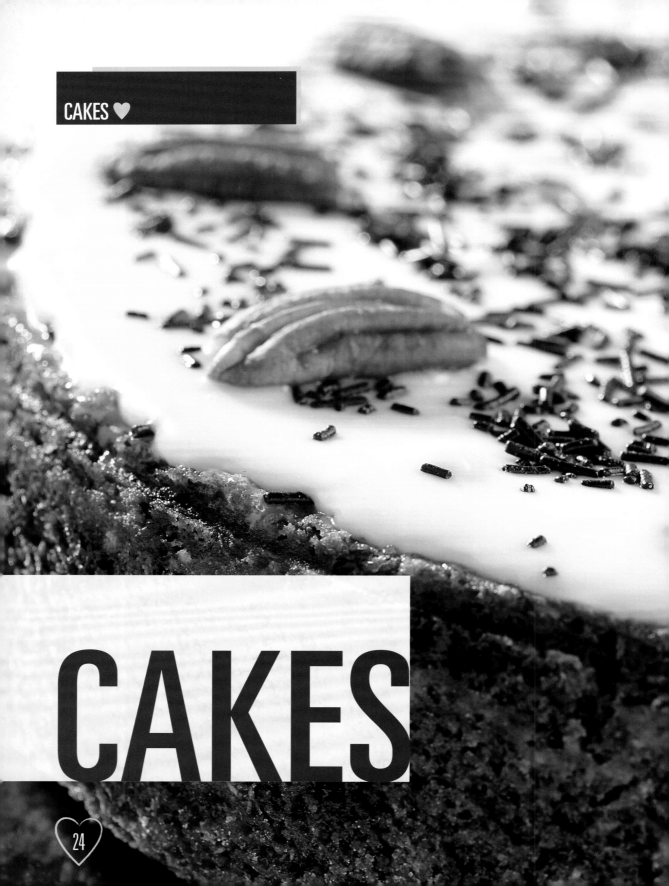

CAKES

CHOCOLATE AND PEANUT BUTTER CUPCAKES

MAKES 12 CUPCAKES

ingredients

25g Salted peanuts
120g Unsalted butter
120g Soft brown sugar
2 Large free-range eggs
40g Buttermilk
100g Self-raising flour
25g Cocoa powder
35g Chocolate chips or callets

BUTTERCREAM TOPPING:

130g Icing sugar
150g Unsalted butter, diced, soft
200g Chunky peanut butter

method

CUPCAKES:

1. Preheat the oven to 160°C.
2. Crush peanuts into small pieces 2 seconds/Speed 4, set aside.
3. Mix all the other cupcake ingredients except the chocolate chips 30 seconds/Speed 4.
4. Scrape down the sides of the TM bowl with the spatula, add the chocolate chips and crushed peanuts, then mix again 10 seconds/Speed 3.
5. Spoon or pipe the mixture into cupcake cases in a muffin tin and fill to three-quarters full.
6. Bake in the oven for 20-25 minutes or until cooked.

BUTTERCREAM TOPPING:

1. Insert Butterfly Whisk, weigh into the TM bowl in order listed the icing sugar, butter and peanut butter, then mix 1 minute/Speed 3.
2. Scrape down the sides of the TM bowl and mix again 2 minutes/Speed 3 until light and fluffy.
3. When the cupcakes are cooled, pipe or spoon on the buttercream topping and garnish with decorations of your choice, e.g. popcorn.

JANIE'S TIP:

Make your own chunky peanut butter by grinding 200g unsalted peanuts with ½ tsp fine sea salt 10 seconds/Speed 10, scraping down the sides of the TM bowl, then blending 30 seconds/Speed 5.

Peanut butter buttercream

CHOCOLATE AND
BLUEBERRY MUFFINS

CHOCOLATE AND
BLUEBERRY MUFFINS

MAKES 8 LARGE OR 12 MEDIUM SIZE MUFFINS

ingredients

150g Fresh or frozen blueberries
150g Chocolate chunks or callets
330g Plain flour
130g Unsalted butter, diced, soft
70g Vegetable oil
110g Icing sugar
1½ tsp Baking powder
1 pinch Fine sea salt
3 Free-range medium eggs
300g Full-fat milk

TO FINISH:

50g Single cream
60g Callebaut 811 NV, 54% dark
    chocolate, small pieces or callets
White chocolate vermicelli, white
    marshmallows or fresh blueberries,
    to decorate

method

1. Place a large bowl on top of the TM lid, weigh into it the blueberries and chocolate chunks then add 1 Tbsp flour. Stir gently to coat the berries and chunks with the flour. Set aside.
2. Weigh the flour, butter, oil and sugar into the TM bowl, add the baking powder and salt then Turbo pulse until crumbs form.
3. Add eggs and milk; knead only 3 or 4 times on the Dough Setting until JUST mixed (batter will still be lumpy).
4. Fold the batter into the floured berries and chocolate chunks by hand until JUST mixed.
5. Gently spoon into a buttered muffin cup pan.
6. Bake the muffins at 180°C for about 25 minutes. Check by inserting a skewer into the muffins – if it comes out clean, the muffins are cooked through. Cool in the pan 5 minutes before taking out to cool completely on a rack. Eat on day of making or freeze as soon as completely cool.

TO FINISH:

1. Warm the cream and dark chocolate 1 minute/50°C/Speed 2 then mix without heat until melted and completely smooth.
2. Spoon some of this glaze over the muffins and decorate with white chocolate vermicelli, little white marshmallows or fresh blueberries as desired.

FRUIT AND
NUT TIFFIN

MAKES 9 LARGE 6CM SQUARES OR 42 SMALL 2.5CM SQUARES

This simple treat is always popular and tends to cause smiles while disappearing quickly.

ingredients

300g Digestive biscuits, broken
25g Roasted hazelnuts
25g Brazil nuts
25g Walnut halves
25g Pecan halves
60g Golden syrup
60g Caramel – see excellent recipe
    for *Sticky Toffee Sauce* in '*Fast and Easy Cooking*'
120g Unsalted butter, diced
280g Dark chocolate 70%, small
    pieces or callets
80g Sultanas
80g Raisins
100g Dried cherries or glacé cherries

method

1. Crush the biscuits 20 seconds/Speed 4 until crumbs. Tip out into a large bowl.
2. Chop the hazelnuts 2 seconds/Speed 5, tip out with the crumbs, then chop the brazil nuts 1 second/Speed 4, tip out with the crumbs, then chop the walnuts and pecans 1 second/Speed 4, tip out with the crumbs.
3. Warm the syrup, caramel, butter and chocolate 2 minutes/50°C/Speed 3 – at this point, about half to three quarters of the chocolate should be melted.
4. Scrape down the sides of the TM bowl and stir 3 minutes/Speed 3 without heat until all the chocolate is melted.
5. Add to the digestive crumbs bowl, add the fruits, and stir well until evenly mixed.
6. Pour onto a greaseproof paper lined tray or loose-bottom cake tin 20x20cm and set in the fridge until firm.
7. Cut into squares or fingers.
8. Squares can be coated on the base with chocolate, fully enrobed or just spun with chocolate to decorate as desired.

JOHN'S TIP

This recipe keeps well and is versatile as it can be presented as a cake slice finger. Cut small it makes a good 'mini bite' or cut even smaller it can make a great addition to your petits fours selection.

DARK TRUFFLE GANACHE CAKE

SERVES 16

ingredients

75g Amaretti biscuits
20g Unsalted butter
440g Venezuela Amedei Chuao, dark chocolate 70%, small
   pieces or callets
50g Madagascar Tanariva, milk chocolate 33%, small pieces
   or callets
70g Liquid glucose
500g Double cream

TO SERVE:

Cocoa powder for dusting
Single cream – optional

method

1. Line a 23cm spring form cake tin with a circle of greaseproof
   or silicone paper and lightly brush the paper and sides of the
   tin with oil.
2. Crush and slightly warm the Amaretti biscuits and butter
   30 seconds/100°C/Speed 4, then press into the base of the tin.
3. Grate both chocolates together 10 seconds/Speed 10, then
   melt 5 minutes/50°C/Speed 3 – it will clump together then
   gradually melt.
4. Meanwhile, heat the glucose in a pan on the hob until it
   starts to bubble then take off the heat.
5. Once the chocolate has all melted, remove the TM lid, scrape
   down the sides of the TM bowl, add the hot glucose to the
   chocolate (avoiding the blade unit) then mix it in at Speed 3
   until completely smooth. Pour out into a large bowl.
6. Insert the Butterfly Whisk in a clean TM bowl and whip the
   cream at Speed 3 JUST until slightly thickened. Fold half into
   the chocolate mixture then fold in the rest.
7. Pour the mixture into the prepared tin. Tap the tin gently to
   even the mixture out. Cover with cling film and chill overnight.
8. Just before serving, run a palette knife around the sides to
   loosen, then transfer to a serving plate and dust the surface
   with sifted cocoa powder.

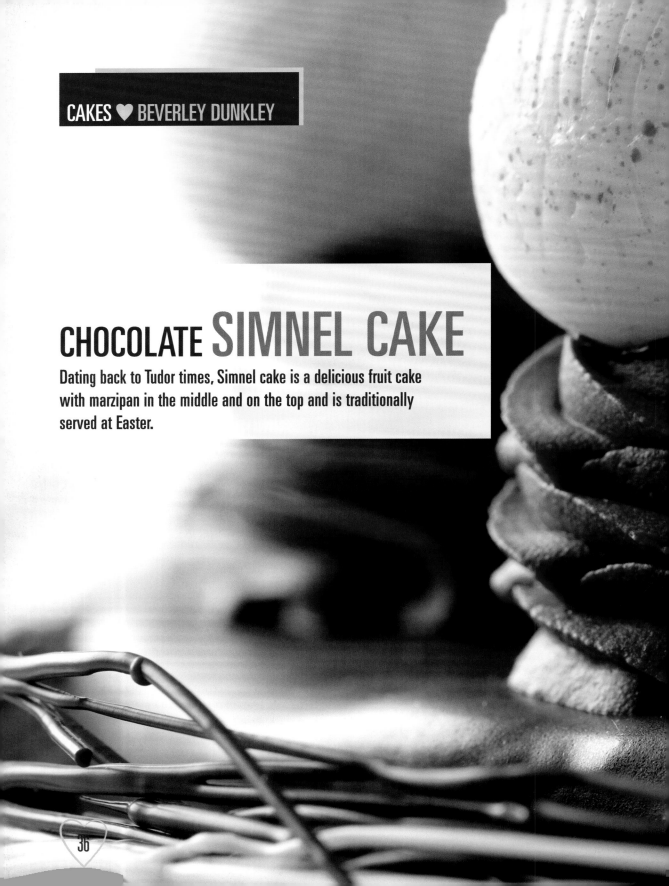

CHOCOLATE SIMNEL CAKE

Dating back to Tudor times, Simnel cake is a delicious fruit cake with marzipan in the middle and on the top and is traditionally served at Easter.

CHOCOLATE SIMNEL CAKE

SERVES 11 OR MORE

ingredients

SIMNEL CAKE:

150g Chopped candied fruit

150g Currants

1 tsp Grated lemon zest

1 tsp Real vanilla extract or vanilla
 paste

30g Brandy

50g Callebaut 811 NV dark chocolate
 54%, small pieces or callets

50g Unsalted butter, diced

3 Free-range large eggs

100g Caster sugar

110g Plain flour

15g Cocoa powder, e.g.
 Cacao Barry Extra Brute

150g Marzipan – see recipe p230

DECORATION:

150g Callebaut 811 NV dark
 chocolate, 54% cocoa solids, small
 pieces or callets

150g Double cream

11 small Easter eggs

NEST DECORATION:

Callebaut 811 NV dark chocolate

Callebaut W2 NV white chocolate

Moulded chocolate hen

method

SIMNEL CAKE:

1. Preheat the oven to 180°C.
2. Line an 18cm round deep cake tin with silicone paper.
3. Place a bowl on top of the TM lid and weigh in the fruits then add the lemon zest, vanilla and brandy; stir then leave to soak for at least 20 minutes.
4. Melt the chocolate and butter 2 minutes/50°C/Speed 3, pausing to scrape down the sides of the TM bowl once or twice, it should be fully melted and smooth – heat 1 minute longer if needed.
5. Add remaining ingredients, mix 30 seconds/Speed 5 then stir into the soaked fruits with the spatula.
6. Pour half the batter into the prepared cake tin.
7. Roll the marzipan into a disc about 18cm diameter x 1cm thick then place it on top of the cake batter.
8. Cover completely with the remaining batter.
9. Bake for approximately 50 minutes until a skewer inserted in the centre comes out clean.

DECORATION:

1. Melt the chocolate and cream in a clean TM bowl 1½ minutes/50°C/Speed 2, pausing to scrape down the TM bowl once, then continue to mix without heat until completely melted and smooth.
2. Spread half the glaze on top of the cake with a palette knife, allowing the glaze to pour off the sides slightly.
3. Cool the rest of the glaze in a bowl until almost fully set, then aerate by hand with a balloon whisk until thick enough to pipe. Transfer to a paper piping cone.
4. Pipe 11 rosettes around the top of the cake and place a small Easter egg on each.

NEST DECORATION:

1. Melt the dark and white chocolate separately at 37°C and place each into a paper piping cone; the chocolate doesn't have to be tempered for this application.
2. Pipe fine long lines of white chocolate onto a frozen granite tile about 20x10cm.
3. Pipe long lines of dark chocolate on top of the white chocolate; the chocolate will set immediately on the frozen granite but remain flexible for a minute or so; lift the chocolate lattice off the tile immediately with a palette knife.
4. Concertina the lattice together and roll while still flexible around the cake to form a nest – you will need approximately three batches of piped lattice to wrap around the complete cake.
5. Decorate the centre of the cake with a moulded chocolate hen.

"IT'S NOT THAT CHOCOLATES ARE A SUBSTITUTE FOR LOVE. LOVE IS A SUBSTITUTE FOR CHOCOLATE. CHOCOLATE IS, LET'S FACE IT, FAR MORE RELIABLE THAN A MAN."

MIRANDA INGRAM

CHOCOLATE MUFFINS

MAKES 10-12 MUFFINS

Super speedy, great for when friends suddenly appear.

ingredients

200g Plain white flour
50g Plain brown flour
1 tsp Bicarbonate of soda
2 Tbsp Cocoa powder
100g Unsalted butter, soft, diced
250g Soft brown sugar
2 Free-range large eggs
130g Sour cream
200g Callebaut 811 NV, 54% dark
    chocolate, small pieces or callets

method

1. Cut baking paper into 15cm squares and push each one into the cavities of a cupcake pan so the sides rise above to make homemade cupcake cases.
2. Preheat the oven to 170°C.
3. Mix all the ingredients 15 seconds/Speed 5.
4. Scrape down the sides of the TM bowl and mix 5 seconds/Speed 5.
5. Spoon in the mix to about half full and bake for 25 minutes or until done – they should be springy to the touch.

CHOCOLATE AND
FRUIT SODA LOAF

CHOCOLATE AND
FRUIT SODA LOAF

MAKES 3 LOAVES USING TINS APPROXIMATELY 21X11CM X 6CM DEEP

This will taste even better the next day — if you have any left! Perfect toasted. Freezes well.

ingredients

40g Dried apricots, halved
40g Sultanas
40g Dried cherries or natural colour glacé cherries
40g Dates, stoneless
20g Goji berries or dried cranberries
50g Brown sugar
130g Dark bake-stable chocolate chunks or callets
120g Bran
50g Porridge oats
50g Wheat germ
350g Plain white flour
270g Wholemeal flour
20g Baking powder
1½ tsp Bicarbonate of soda
2 tsp Fine sea salt
2 Free-range large eggs
50g Honey
1 litre Buttermilk
25g Pumpkin seeds to sprinkle on top

TO SERVE:

Butter
Chocolate spread — see recipe page p200
Chocolate hazelnut spread — see recipe in 'Fast and Easy Cooking'

method

1. Place a very large bowl on the lid of the TM bowl and weigh into it the fruits, sugar, chocolate chunks and dry ingredients. Set aside.

2. Mix the eggs, honey and buttermilk 30 seconds/ Speed 8 and pour into the same large bowl.

3. Mix well using a wooden spoon then spoon into greased and floured baking tins.

4. Sprinkle the tops with pumpkin seeds and bake at 160°C for 60-75 minutes until a skewer inserted into the centre comes out clean.

5. Cool 5 minutes in the tins, then remove and cool completely on a rack before slicing.

46

SACHER TORTE

MAKES 1 CAKE 18CM ROUND

It's amazing to think that with your Thermomix you can produce a cake of this standard at home!

ingredients

SPONGE:

220g Free-range egg whites, about
   6 to 7 large
130g Granulated sugar
150g Free-range egg yolks,
   about 8 to 9 large
150g Unsalted butter, diced, soft
150g Callebaut 811 NV, 54% dark
   chocolate, small pieces or callets
70g Plain flour
1 tsp Baking powder
150g Ground almonds

GANACHE:

300g Double cream
60g Granulated sugar
300g Callebaut 811 NV, 54% dark
   chocolate, small pieces or callets
60g Unsalted butter, diced
60g Liquid glucose, warmed in a pan
   on the hob until bubbling

method

SPONGE:

1. Insert the Butterfly Whisk in a clean and grease-free TM bowl then whisk the egg whites and sugar 7 minutes/70°C/Speed 3 – you will have a thick glossy meringue.
2. Add the egg yolks and mix 10 seconds/Speed 3.
3. Set a dish on top of the TM lid and weigh into it the chocolate and butter. Do the same in another dish with the flour, baking powder and ground almonds.
4. Insert a jam funnel into the hole in the TM lid , turn the TM to Speed 3 and very gradually add the butter dice through the hole in the TM lid, followed by the chocolate. Keep mixing until you can hear that it's all melted and smooth.
5. Turn down to Speed 2 and slowly add the dry ingredients.
6. Pour into a buttered and floured 18cm loose-bottom cake tin and bake at 180°C for about 30-40 minutes.
7. Leave in tin for 10 minutes then remove to a wire rack and cool completely.
8. Cut it in half and sandwich together with warmed apricot jam.
9. Mask the cake (brush it) with warmed apricot jam and then glaze with ganache.

GANACHE:

1. Warm the cream, sugar, chocolate and butter 2 minutes/50°C/Speed 3, pausing halfway to scrape down the sides of the TM bowl with the spatula. About half the chocolate should be melted by now.
2. Add the hot glucose and mix 3 minutes/Speed 3 without heat until the chocolate is fully melted and smooth, pausing once or twice to scrape down the sides of the TM bowl.

3. Remove TM lid and test with a temperature probe – it should read 32°C to 34°C. If it's warmer than that, add 30g chocolate at a time until the temperature is correct, melting it fully each time before probing – this will give you a perfectly glossy tempered ganache.

4. Pour over the cake and allow to set – for a classic Sacher Torte look, pipe a curly capital "S" onto the top of the cake once the ganache has set.

Chocolate sponge mix

GLUTEN-FREE
HEAVENLY CHOCOLATE CAKE

SERVES 8-10

This utterly beautiful cake is much easier to make than you might think at first glance.
You will definitely impress your friends, family and guests when you present this for dessert!

ingredients

GLUTEN-FREE CHOCOLATE SPONGE:

180g Free-range egg whites,
 5 to 6 large
190g Caster sugar
120g Free-range egg yolks,
 7 to 8 large
50g Cocoa powder, sieved

CHOCOLATE MOUSSE:

200g 33% milk chocolate, e.g.
 Callebaut 823 NV, small pieces or
 callets
250g Whipping cream

**VANILLA MOUSSE AND
RASPBERRIES:**

60g Caster sugar
50g Free-range egg yolks, about
 3 large
250g Full-fat milk
½ Vanilla pod, seeds only
2 leaves Gelatine
250g Whipping cream
1 handful Raspberries, fresh or frozen

TO FINISH:

Neutral glaze – optional
Chocolate decorations – optional

method

GLUTEN-FREE CHOCOLATE SPONGE:

1. Insert the Butterfly Whisk and whisk the
    egg whites with the caster sugar
    7 minutes/Speed 3 – you will have a stiff
    and glossy meringue.
2. Add the egg yolks and mix 10 seconds/
    Speed 3.
3. Place a jam funnel into the hole of the
    TM lid, add the cocoa powder through it,
    mix 10 seconds/Speed 3 then scrape down
    the sides of the TM bowl and mix again
    2 seconds/Speed 3.
4. Spread onto a lined 40x60cm tray and bake
    the sponge about 12 minutes at 190°C.

CHOCOLATE MOUSSE:

1. Insert Butterfly Whisk in a clean TM bowl
    and whip 500g cream at Speed 3 until
    JUST softly whipped. Transfer half to one
    large bowl and half to another large bowl
    (you'll use the second bowl of whipped
    cream for the vanilla mousse).
2. Melt the chocolate in the rinsed and dried
    TM bowl 4 minutes/37°C/Speed 1, pausing
    once to scrape down the sides of the
    TM bowl.
3. Scrape down again and finish the melting
    2 minutes/Speed 2 without heat.

4. Fold half the chocolate into one bowl of whipped cream, then fold in the rest of the chocolate until no streaks remain – this is your chocolate mousse.
5. Line a 20x20cm frame or loose-bottomed cake tin with half the sponge (cut to fit) and top with the chocolate mousse followed by another layer of sponge.

VANILLA MOUSSE AND RASPBERRIES:

1. Cook the sugar, egg yolks, milk and vanilla seeds 7 minutes/80°C/Speed 4. Meanwhile, soak the gelatine in cold water.
2. Add the drained gelatine leaves and mix

10 seconds/Speed 4. Pour out into a large bowl and set aside to cool.
3. Fold the cooled custard mix into the reserved bowl of whipped cream – you may need to use a hand whisk to stir in the last few bits of whipped cream.
4. Pour on top of the second sponge layer then add the raspberries (fresh or frozen are fine) and place in a freezer or fridge until set.

TO FINISH:

1. Glaze with a neutral glaze.
2. Finish with chocolate decorations.

CHOCOLATE CHIP AND
BANANA LOAF

ENOUGH TO FILL A 1KG LOAF TIN OR 2 SMALLER LOAF TINS

ingredients

90g Dark chocolate 80%, small pieces
or callets, divided 50g and 40g

70g Butter, diced, soft

130g Ripe bananas, weighed after
skins removed (about 2 small to
medium)

120g Soft brown sugar

2 Free-range large eggs

100g Plain flour

1½ tsp Baking powder

25g Cocoa powder

25g Flaked almonds

Cocoa powder, for dusting

Orange curd, to serve

method

1. Preheat the oven to 170°C.
2. Line a 1kg loaf tin with greaseproof paper.
3. Melt 50g chocolate with the butter 3 minutes/50°C/Speed 3
   or longer until completely melted and smooth, pausing once
   or twice to scrape down the sides of the TM bowl with the
   spatula.
4. Add all remaining ingredients except the 40g chocolate and
   the flaked almonds, then mix 30 seconds/Speed 5.
5. Scrape down, add the remaining chocolate and stir in at
   Speed 3 for a few seconds.
6. Spoon into the loaf tin, sprinkle with the almonds and bake
   in the middle of the oven for around 45-60 minutes or until a
   skewer comes out clean from the centre of the cake.
7. When cooked dust with cocoa powder and leave to cool.
8. Serve with orange curd.

JANIE'S TIP:

Orange curd can easily be made in your Thermomix – see Lemon
Curd recipe in *'Fast and Easy Cooking'* and use the recipe as a
"guideline" – do the triple recipe and use 1 large or 2 medium
juicy oranges and half a small lemon instead of 3 lemons.

CHOCOLATE CUPCAKES DECORATED WITH A
CHOCOLATE NEST AND MINI CHOCOLATE EGGS

MAKES 12 CUPCAKES

These little cupcakes are lovely with their Easter decorations, and are equally delicious plain for a quick after school treat.

ingredients

CUPCAKES:

120g Self-raising flour
25g Cocoa powder, e.g.
   Cacao Barry Extra Brute
150g Butter, diced, soft
150g Free-range eggs, weighed
   without shells (about 3 large)
150g Granulated sugar

CHOCOLATE GLAZE:

220g Double cream
220g Callebaut 811 NV, 54%
   dark chocolate, small pieces or
   callets

DECORATION:

220g Callebaut 811 NV, 54%
   dark chocolate, small pieces or
   callets, melted
Mini chocolate eggs

method

CUPCAKES:

1. Insert the Butterfly Whisk, add all the cupcake ingredients in order listed, then mix 30 seconds/ Speed 5.
2. Scrape down the sides of the TM bowl with the spatula and mix again 30 seconds/ Speed 5.
3. Pipe or spoon into individual paper cases three-quarters full.
4. Bake at 180°C for 13-15 minutes.

CHOCOLATE GLAZE:

1. When the cakes are cool and you're ready to decorate them, prepare the chocolate glaze by heating the cream and chocolate in a clean TM bowl 4 minutes/37°C/ Speed 2.
2. Scrape down the sides and stir without heat at Speed 2 to melt the remaining bits of chocolate – it should end up completely smooth.

ASSEMBLY:

1. Cut the top off each cooled cupcake at an angle.
2. Pour half the chocolate glaze into a small bowl. Aerate the other half with a balloon whisk until very thick, then pipe onto the cupcake with a star nozzle.
3. Replace the top of the cupcake and dip upside down in the liquid glaze to give a shiny, even coating.
4. For the nest decoration, place melted dark chocolate into a paper piping cone and pipe a fine lattice of lines on a frozen granite tile – about 20x10cm.
5. Lift the chocolate lattice off the tile immediately with a palette knife, then concertina the lattice together and shape while still flexible to form a nest.
6. Place the chocolate nest immediately on each chocolate cupcake to stick to the setting glaze.
7. Finish the decoration with three mini chocolate eggs.

CHOCOLATE AND COFFEE CAKE

This is a simple and elegant cake, perfect for a coffee morning or any time.

56

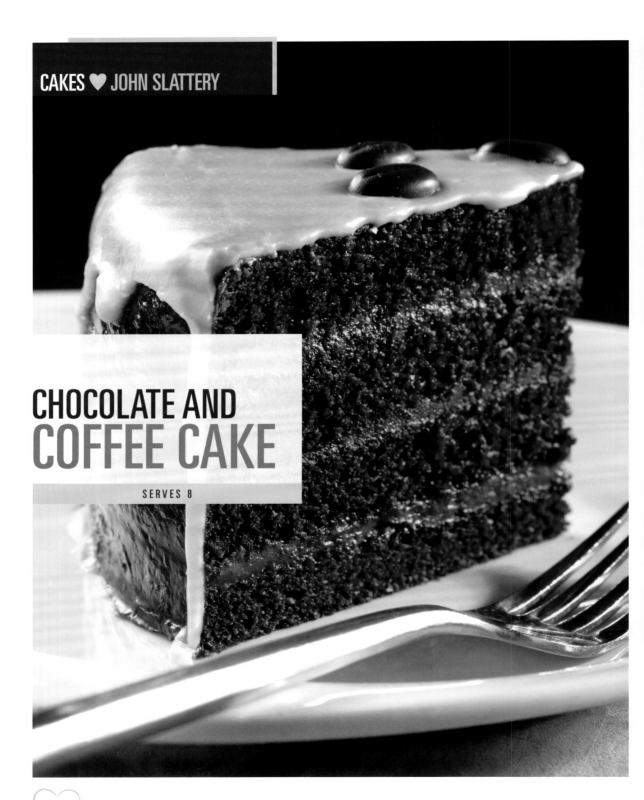

CHOCOLATE AND
COFFEE CAKE

SERVES 8

ingredients

COFFEE CUSTARD:

250g Granulated sugar
20g Instant coffee granules
380g Water
100g Corn flour
45g Unsalted butter, diced
30g Golden syrup

CAKE:

100g Unsalted butter, diced
200g Granulated sugar
2 Free-range large eggs
45g Cocoa powder
1¼ tsp Baking powder
1 tsp Bicarbonate of soda
1 pinch Fine sea salt
170g Plain flour
160g Full-fat milk

COFFEE ICING:

120g Icing sugar
20g Boiling water
A few instant coffee granules to add
flavour and colour

DECORATION:

Chocolate coffee beans

Coffee custard

method

CUSTARD:

1. Cook all custard ingredients 9 minutes/90°C/Speed 4.
2. Taste to check the corn flour is cooked; cook 2 minutes longer if desired.
3. Pour into a bowl, cover with cling film and chill in the refrigerator until cold and firm.

CAKE:

1. Mix all cake ingredients 30 seconds/Speed 5.
2. Scrape down the sides of the TM bowl with the spatula and mix again a few seconds/Speed 5.
3. Divide the mix between two greased 18cm cake tins.
4. Bake in a pre-heated oven at 170°C for 25-30 minutes.

ASSEMBLY:

1. Cut the top crust off both cakes to create flat tops, then split each cake into two discs. (Freeze the leftover round cake tops to use in other recipes, e.g. Drunken Chocolate Cake p74.)
1. Just before assembling the cake, return the cold custard to the TM bowl and mix at Speed 5 while stirring with the TM spatula through the hole in the TM lid until completely smooth and spreadable.
2. Spread approximately 30 per cent of the custard onto each disc of cake as you stack the first three layers, then top with the fourth disc.
3. Brush the remaining custard around the sides and top to seal the cake with a very thin layer of custard.
4. Mix the icing ingredients together and pour over the top of the cake, allowing it to flow down the sides here and there.
5. To complete, sprinkle with a few chocolate-covered coffee beans.

JANIE'S TIP:

This cake is also delicious without the icing.

SWISS FOREST GATEAU

SWISS FOREST GATEAU

SERVES 8

ingredients

CHOCOLATE CHANTILLY:

500g Whipping cream
50g Caster sugar
65g 70% dark chocolate, small pieces
  or callets
25g Cocoa block, chopped

CHOCOLATE SPONGE SHEET:

Enough for 3x18cm rounds to make
  one gateau
60g Corn flour
60g Plain flour
50g Cocoa powder
250g Caster sugar
250g Free-range egg whites
230g Free-range egg yolks

KIRSCH SYRUP:

100g Stock syrup – see recipe p88
25g Water
Kirsch, to taste (approximately 20g)

ASSEMBLY:

Morello cherries, in juice
Callebaut W2 NV white chocolate,
  melted
Arrowroot or cornflour, as required
Whipped cream – optional
Cocoa powder and/or icing sugar

♡

method

CHOCOLATE CHANTILLY CREAM:

1. Heat the cream, sugar, chocolate and cocoa block 3 minutes/50°C/Speed 3, pausing once or twice to scrape down the sides of the TM bowl with the spatula.
2. Scrape down again and mix 3 minutes/Speed 3 without heat until completely melted and smooth.
3. Store in the refrigerator for 12-18 hours before use.

CHOCOLATE SPONGE SHEET:

1. Sieve together the flours and cocoa powder by Turbo pulsing a few times then tip out and set aside.
2. Insert the Butterfly Whisk into a clean and grease-free TM bowl (or you could use your second TM bowl for this if you have one) and whisk the sugar and egg whites 9 minutes/37°C/Speed 3 – you will have a stiff glossy meringue.
3. Stir in the egg yolks 10 seconds/Speed 3.

4. Place a jam funnel into the hole in the TM lid then turn to Speed 2 and add the cocoa/flour mix; scrape down the sides of the TM bowl and finish with another few seconds at Speed 2.
5. Spread mix on to a silicone paper lined tray 40x60cm and bake at 200°C for 8-10 minutes. Alternatively, bake in 3x18cm spring form or loose-bottom cake tins.

KIRSCH SYRUP:

1. Weigh all ingredients into a jug placed on the lid of the TM bowl and mix together.

ASSEMBLY:

1. Cut the sponge into three 18cm diameter circles.
2. Place one sponge into an 18cm ring or spring form cake tin lined with silicone paper or acetate on the base and sides and pipe the first layer of chocolate chantilly over the sponge.
3. Place a second sponge onto the cream then brush on some Kirsch syrup.

62

4. Pipe a second layer of Chantilly on it and sprinkle with some halved morello cherries.

5. Cover with a third sponge, brush with kirsch syrup and cover with a thin layer of Chantilly.

6. Chill or blast freeze and when firm remove the ring.

7. Thinly spread melted white chocolate on to a frozen piece of marble or frozen steel tray then quickly lift off with a flat knife. Place a band of chocolate around the gateau and place some on top.

8. Heat some of the cherry juice and thicken with arrowroot or corn flour, add the rest of the cherries (whole) and once the cherries and sauce are cool, place them in the centre of the gateau in a 6-8cm circle.

9. Decorate the edge with Chantilly or cream and dust with a little cocoa powder and/or icing sugar.

"THERE'S NOTHING BETTER THAN A GOOD FRIEND, EXCEPT A GOOD FRIEND WITH CHOCOLATE."

LINDA GRAYSON, "THE PICKWICK PAPERS"

GINGER AND CHOCOLATE CAKE

MAKES ENOUGH FOR A 1KG LOAF TIN OR 8-10 MINI LOAVES

For those who love ginger this is a must-try recipe!

ingredients

- 100g 54% dark chocolate, e.g. Callebaut 811 NV, small pieces or callets
- 250g Ginger beer
- 250g Plain flour
- 50g Cocoa powder
- 1½ tsp Bicarbonate of soda
- 140g Granulated sugar
- 1 tsp Ground ginger
- 40g Vegetable oil or butter
- 40g Stem ginger, finely chopped

method

1. Preheat the oven to 170°C.
2. Line a 1kg loaf tin with greaseproof paper or if using mini-loaf tins butter them and dredge with flour.
3. Melt the chocolate with the ginger beer 5 minutes/50°C/Speed 3 until completely melted.
4. Add the oil, stem ginger and dry ingredients then mix 20 seconds/Speed 5, pausing to scrape down once, and when all incorporated pour into the lined cake tin or mini loaf tins.
5. Turn to Speed 10 for 2 seconds to flick all remaining batter from the blades onto the sides of the TM bowl, then add this to the tin/s.
6. Bake large loaf about 30-40 minutes or until cooked – springy to the touch and a skewer inserted in the centre comes out clean. Small loaves will take 10-15 minutes.

WHITE CHOCOLATE
CARROT CAKE

MAKES A 24CM DIAMETER CAKE, SERVES 10 TO 12

ingredients

200g Butter, diced, soft
250g Caster sugar
1 tsp Real vanilla extract
150g Plain white flour
75g Wholemeal flour
1¼ tsp Bicarbonate of soda
1½ tsp Baking powder
1 pinch Fine sea salt
1 to 2 tsp Ground cinnamon
   (TM ground has best flavour)
3 Free-range large eggs
300g Carrots, cut into 3 cm chunks
100g Pecan nuts or walnuts
100g White chocolate, e.g. Callebaut
   W2 NV, small pieces or callets

TO FINISH:

100g Single cream
120g White chocolate, e.g. Callebaut
   W2 NV, small pieces or callets
Pecans or walnuts, to decorate
   (dependent on those used in the
   cake)
Strawberry or raspberry sauce,
   to serve
Whipped cream, to serve

method

1. Weigh all ingredients except chocolate chunks into the TM bowl in order listed.
2. Mix 40 seconds/Speed 5 while stirring with the TM spatula through the hole in the TM lid. Check all the carrot chunks have disappeared; mix a little longer at Speed 5 if required.
3. Add chocolate chunks and stir in by hand with the TM spatula.
4. Pour the mix into a greased 23cm spring form mould/tin and bake at 175°C for 40-50 minutes. Check with a skewer – if the cake is cooked, the skewer should come out clean. Allow the cake to cool before taking it out of the mould.

TO FINISH:

1. Heat the cream and white chocolate in a clean TM bowl 2 minutes/50°C/Speed 2½.
2. Scrape down the sides of the TM bowl then continue mixing at Speed 2 without heat until smooth.
3. Spread this glaze over the top of the carrot cake and decorate with either pecans or walnuts.
4. Serve with a strawberry or raspberry sauce and softly whipped cream.

ROYALE

SERVES 8-10

You will definitely feel as if you have created a cake fit for royalty when you make this! Impressive looks and wonderful flavour.

ingredients

SPONGE:

340g Icing sugar
180g Ground almonds
190g Ground hazelnuts
560g Egg whites
130g Caster sugar
190g Full-fat milk
100g Plain flour

PRALINE BASE:

200g Feuilletine –
  see recipe p226
130g White
chocolate,
  e.g. Callebaut W2 NV, small pieces or
  callets
500g Praline paste –
  see recipe p231

CHOCOLATE MOUSSE:

250g milk chocolate, small pieces
  or callets
500g Whipping cream

TO FINISH:

Chocolate for spraying or icing
  sugar and cocoa powder
Chocolate decorations

method

SPONGE:

1. Sieve the icing sugar, grind almonds and the hazelnuts by Turbo pulsing a few times; tip out and set aside.
2. In a clean and grease-free TM bowl, insert the Butterfly Whisk and whisk the egg whites and caster sugar 7 minutes/37°C/Speed 3 – it will form a stiff glossy meringue.
3. Add the milk and mix in 10 seconds/Speed 3.
4. Place a jam funnel into the hole in the TM lid, turn to Speed 3 and gradually add in the nut mixture followed by the flour, then pause to scrape down the sides of the TM bowl before finishing at Speed 3 for a few seconds.
5. Spread onto a 40x60cm tray lined with baking paper and bake at 190°C for about 15 minutes.

PRALINE LAYER:

1. Set a large bowl on top of the TM lid, press the scales to zero, weigh the feuilletine into it then set aside.
2. Melt the white chocolate in a clean TM bowl 2 minutes/50°C/Speed 3, add the praline paste, mix 15 seconds/Speed 3 then stir into the feuilletine.
3. Line a 20x20cm frame or loose-bottomed cake tin with the sponge (cut to fit). Spread the praline mixture on top of the sponge.

CHOCOLATE MOUSSE:

1. Melt the milk chocolate 4 minutes/37°C/Speed 3 then scrape down the sides of the TM bowl and continue melting 2 minutes/Speed 2 without heat. Pour into a large bowl and set aside.
2. Insert the Butterfly Whisk into a clean TM bowl and whip the cream at Speed 3 until JUST lightly whipped.
3. Fold half the cream into the melted chocolate then fold in the rest until no streaks remain; pour into the frame on top of the praline and sponge.
4. Chill in the freezer or fridge until set.

TO FINISH:

1. Use a warmed palette knife to loosen the edges of the cake before removing from the tin/frame, then spray with a chocolate spray gun or dust with a mixture of icing sugar and cocoa powder.
2. Add some chocolate decorations to finish.

JANIE'S TIPS:

Praline paste (see p231) is easy to make and takes only 15 or 20 minutes. Feuilletine (see p226) is also easy to make and it's worthwhile because it tastes so good.

71

RICH CHOCOLATE
FRUIT CAKE

MAKES A 20CM ROUND CAKE

ingredients

350g Currants
150g Sultanas
150g Raisins
70g Dried cherries
1 Organic orange, zest and juice
100g Chocolate liqueur
170g Unsalted butter, diced, soft
170g Soft dark brown sugar
3 Free-range large eggs
2 Tbsp Molasses
175g Plain flour
40g Cocoa powder
1 tsp Ground cinnamon
1 tsp Ground ginger
100g Dark chocolate, chips or callets
50g Ground hazelnuts
Chocolate marzipan, to decorate –
   see recipe p230
Chocolate sugar paste – optional

method

1. Set a large bowl on top of the TM lid, set scales to zero, weigh in the fruits, add the orange zest, juice and liqueur. Stir well then cover and leave for 24 hours to marinate.
2. Preheat the oven to 150°C. Line a 20cm round cake tin with a double lining of greaseproof paper.
3. Mix the butter, sugar, eggs, molasses, flour, cocoa, cinnamon, ginger, chocolate chips and hazelnuts 30 seconds/Speed 5 while stirring through the hole in the TM lid with the TM spatula.
4. Add the soaked fruit and stir in at Speed 3/Reverse Blade Direction, using the TM spatula to help as needed.
5. Spoon the mix into the tin and bake for 2-2½ hours or until a skewer inserted in the centre of the cake comes out clean (if the top of the cake becomes too dark during cooking place a piece of greaseproof paper on top).
6. When the cake has cooled completely, remove from tin, coat with chocolate marzipan and chocolate sugar paste then decorate for any occasion.

JANIE'S TIP:
Grind your own hazelnuts 10 seconds/Speed 10.

DRUNKEN CHOCOLATE CAKE

SERVES 12

This is one of those recipes that tastes far better than it reads. It creates a rich, moist dessert that if served with a dollop of freshly whipped cream is a simple but elegant finale to any meal. Make one day ahead.

ingredients

170g Chocolate cake, broken into small pieces
100g Brandy
170g Digestive biscuits, broken
140g Fresh whipping cream
400g 54% dark chocolate, e.g. Callebaut 811 NV, small pieces or callets

DECORATION:

100g Digestive biscuit crumbs, sieved to remove fine particles

method

1. Line the base and sides of a 25cm cake ring or spring form tin with acetate or greaseproof paper.
2. Crush the biscuits by hand – you want small pieces, not crumbs.
3. Crumb the chocolate cake pieces for a few seconds at Speed 4 and tip out into a bowl, then place the bowl on top of the TM lid and weigh in the brandy; set aside for at least 5 minutes to absorb, stirring occasionally to make sure all the cake is moist.
4. Heat the cream 5 minutes/ 100°C/Speed 2, then add the chocolate and stir at Speed 3 until completely melted and smooth.
5. Add the soaked cake and biscuit pieces then stir 30 seconds/Speed 3/Reverse Blade Direction.
6. Fill the prepared cake ring and place into the refrigerator overnight.
7. Remove from the refrigerator, remove the metal ring or tin and peel away the acetate strip.

DECORATION:

1. Use a heat gun or a hair dryer to warm the surface of the cake.
2. Press the biscuit crumbs around the sides and over the top.
3. Mark with the back of a knife blade into portions.

JOHN'S NOTES:

1. Most other spirits or liqueurs can be substituted for the brandy; Amaretto, Grand Marnier, Baileys Irish Cream or a mellow whisky all work well.
2. The flavour of this cake improves with maturing for a day or two in an airtight container in a cool place, before final decoration and serving.

ALMOND, POLENTA
AND CHOCOLATE CAKES

MAKES 12 INDIVIDUAL CAKES

These little moist cakes are fast and easy with your Thermomix, and will keep well for up to 5 days in an airtight container, but only if you hide them. They can be made gluten-free simply by using GF baking powder.

ingredients

100g Granulated sugar
300g Almonds, whole
1 Organic orange, thin peelings of the zest and 25g of the freshly squeezed juice
100g Polenta
1½ tsp Baking powder or gluten-free baking powder
250g Salted butter, diced, soft
3 Free-range medium eggs
25g Buttermilk
230g Mixed dried fruit of choice: sultanas, chopped apricots, goji berries, cranberries, candied peel
100g Small bake-stable dark chocolate chips (see note) or dark chocolate callets
Icing sugar, to serve

method

1. Grind sugar, almonds and orange peelings 10 seconds/ Speed 10.
2. Add the orange juice, polenta, baking powder, butter, eggs and buttermilk then mix 30 seconds/Speed 5 while stirring with the TM spatula through the hole in the TM lid.
3. Scrape down the sides of the TM bowl and mix again 5 seconds/Speed 4.
4. Add fruit and chocolate chips then mix 15 seconds/ Speed 3/Reverse Blade Direction, while stirring with the TM spatula through the hole in the TM lid.
5. Spoon (three quarters full) into silicone cake moulds or large muffin moulds about 8cm circumference x 4cm deep.
6. Bake at 165°C for about 30 minutes.
7. Cool in the silicone moulds then take out the cakes and dust with icing sugar before serving.
8. Store in an air-tight container or freeze.

DIRK'S NOTE:

Bake-stable chocolate chips don't melt in oven temperatures of up to 200°C and are ideal to add to bread, croissants, brioches, cakes or pastry bases. Bake-stable chocolate comes in a wide variety of shapes and sizes from sticks to small drops and large chunks, and in milk, white and dark chocolate. If you don't have any, use regular chocolate chips or callets instead.

76

ORIGINE

MAKES ONE 20CM CAKE

I'm running out of superlatives to describe these wonderful chocolate recipes - this is another fabulous creation from Thierry Dumouchel that is surprisingly easy to make, very impressive to serve, and so good to eat.

ingredients

SPONGE:

280g Free-range egg whites (9 to 10 large)
100g Caster sugar
300g Ground almonds
260g Free-range egg yolks (approx 10 large)
75g Butter, diced and soft
60g Cocoa powder
130g Plain flour

DARK AND MILK CHOCOLATE MOUSSES:

450g Stock syrup – see recipe p88
220g Free-range egg yolks (approx 9 large)
370g Tanzania 70% dark chocolate, small pieces or callets
1500g Whipping cream, divided 750g and 750g

450g Papouasie or 35% milk chocolate, small pieces or callets

GLAZE:

250g Full-fat milk
200g Callebaut 811 NV, 54% dark chocolate, small pieces or callets
150g Stock syrup – see recipe p88

200g 80% Dark chocolate, small pieces or callets

TO FINISH:

Chocolate shapes and curls

method

SPONGE:

1. Sieve the cocoa powder and flour by Turbo pulsing a few times. Tip out and set aside.
2. Insert the Butterfly Whisk into a clean and grease-free TM bowl then whisk the egg whites with the sugar 8 minutes/Speed 3 into a glossy meringue. Tip out and set aside (or leave in this TM bowl and use your second TM bowl for the next step).
3. Mix the ground almonds,

egg yolks, butter and cocoa powder at Speed 4 until a paste. Tip out into a large bowl.

4. Stir one third of the meringue into the almond cocoa paste, then gently fold in the rest of the meringue.
5. Add the flour/cocoa mix and fold in gently.
6. Bake at 190°C for 20 minutes in a 20cm round tin lined with greaseproof paper.

CHOCOLATE MOUSSE:

1. Heat the syrup and egg yolks 7 minutes/60°C/Speed 4.
2. Place a large bowl on top of the TM lid and weigh in the dark chocolate, pour half the cooked egg mixture over the chocolate and whisk by hand until the chocolate is melted and the mixture is cooled to room temperature.
3. Meanwhile, weigh the milk chocolate into the TM bowl with the remaining egg mixture

and stir 15 minutes/Speed 3
with the Measuring Cup OFF
until the chocolate is melted
and the mixture is cooled a
little. Pour out into another
large bowl and set aside.

4. Insert Butterfly Whisk into
a clean TM bowl and lightly
whip all the cream at
Speed 3, watching carefully
through the hole in the TM lid.
Stop as soon as it looks JUST
softly whipped on top (it will
be thicker underneath).

5. Add half the whipped cream to
the dark chocolate and half to
the milk chocolate, then fold in

until evenly mixed.

6. Cut the sponge in half and
place one layer in the bottom
of a 20cm cake ring or loose-
bottom cake tin. Pour the dark
chocolate mousse over the
sponge then top with the other
half of the sponge.

7. Pour in the milk chocolate
mousse as a top layer, smooth
with a palette knife then place
in the freezer until set.

GLAZE:

1. Melt the glaze ingredients
4 minutes/50°C/Speed 3,
pausing to scrape down the

sides of the TM bowl once
or twice – about half to two
thirds of the chocolate should
be melted by now – then stir at
Speed 3 without heat until fully
melted and tempered.

2. Remove the cake from the
ring/tin.

3. Place the cake on a wire rack
set on a tray to catch the drips,
then pour the glaze over the
cake and let it run over the
sides.

TO FINISH:

Decorate with chocolate shapes
and curls.

79

CONFECTIONERY

TRUFFLE MEN

MAKES 15-20

Get the children involved and have fun fashioning these little truffle men! And by the way, these ganaches may well become two of your favourites — they are certainly in that category for me — they are fabulous.

ingredients

RASPBERRY GANACHE:

makes enough for 30 to 40 shells

100g Raspberry purée, seedless —
    see fruit purée recipe on p228
60g Whipping cream
180g Callebaut 811 NV, 54% dark
    chocolate, small pieces or callets
15 to 20g Brandy to taste
1 tsp Raspberry eau de vie – optional
20g Liquid glucose

COFFEE GANACHE:

makes enough for 30 to 40 shells

100g Whipping cream
2 level tsp Instant coffee, best quality
200g Callebaut W2 NV white
    chocolate, small pieces or callets
20g Liquid glucose

ASSEMBLY:

Truffle shells (white, milk, dark)
Melted chocolate
Tempered chocolate
Chocolate discs
Marzipan – see recipe on p230
Royal icing
200g Callebaut W2 NV white
    chocolate, small pieces or callets

method

RASPBERRY GANACHE:

1. Heat the purée, cream, chocolate, brandy and eau de vie 2 minutes/50°C/Speed 3, pausing once to scrape down the sides of the TM bowl.
2. Meanwhile, heat the glucose in a small pan until bubbling then remove from the heat and let the bubbles subside.
3. Add the warmed glucose to the TM bowl, avoiding the blade unit.
4. Scrape down again and mix 2 minutes/Speed 3 without heat - it should be completely melted and smooth.
5. Homogenise the ganache by mixing 30 seconds/Speed 4, then transfer to a piping bag.
6. Use at 27°C for filling shells.

COFFEE GANACHE:

1. Heat the cream, coffee and chocolate 1½ minutes/50°C/Speed 3, pausing once to scrape down the sides of the TM bowl.

Coffee ganache

2. Meanwhile, heat the glucose in a small pan until bubbling then remove from the heat and let the bubbles subside.
3. Add the warmed glucose to the TM bowl, avoiding the blade unit.
4. Scrape down again and mix 2 minutes/Speed 3 without heat – it should be completely melted and smooth.
5. Homogenise the ganache by mixing 30 seconds/ Speed 4, then transfer to a piping bag.
6. Use at 27°C for filling shells.

ASSEMBLY:

1. Fill the white and milk shells with coffee ganache and the dark shells with raspberry ganache.
2. Seal the filled shells with melted chocolate and stick two together.
3. Place onto a chocolate disc and allow to set.
4. Pipe out 1.5cm-2cm diameter dots of tempered chocolate onto a flat surface to use as the 'berets'.
5. Decorate the top shell as a face using marzipan or royal icing and place the beret on top.

MILK CHOCOLATE MINT BARS AND
DARK CHOCOLATE CHILLI BARS

Cocoa butter is a fantastic carrier of flavour and can be used to infuse flavour successfully into chocolate bars as Beverley Dunkley does beautifully in these two chocolate bar flavours. Her inspiration for these bars came from recipes featured in Jean Pierre Wybauw's book *"Fine Chocolates 2 – Great Ganache Experience"*. Enjoy the natural flavours!

MAKES 5 X 100g BARS

ingredients

MILK CHOCOLATE FLAVOURED WITH FRESH MINT:

10g Fresh mint leaves
25g Cocoa butter
500g 33% milk chocolate, e.g. Callebaut 823 NV, small pieces or callets

DARK CHOCOLATE FLAVOURED WITH CRUSHED POWDERED CHILLIES:

1 tsp Ground chillies
25g Cocoa butter, melted
500g 54% dark chocolate, e.g. Callebaut 811 NV, small pieces or callets

method

1. Drop the pre-weighed mint leaves onto the running blades at Speed 10 to mince.
2. Scrape down the sides of the TM bowl with the spatula, then add the cocoa butter in small lumps and heat 7 minutes/60°C/Speed 2. Pour out into a small dish, cover and leave to rest overnight at room temperature.
3. In a clean TM bowl, melt the second amount of cocoa butter with the ground chillies (same method) and pour out into another small dish, covering and resting overnight as above.
4. The next day, melt one of the flavoured cocoa butters 1 minute/50°C/Speed 2 and strain. Return to the clean TM bowl with the appropriate chocolate and melt 3 minutes/50°C/Speed 3 for milk chocolate or 4 minutes/50°C/Speed 3 for dark chocolate.
5. Scrape down the sides of the TM bowl with the spatula and finish melting 3 minutes/Speed 2 without heat – the chocolate should be completely melted and smooth and between 30°C and 31°C on a temperature probe for milk chocolate or between 32°C and 34°C for dark chocolate, i.e. tempered.
6. Pour into chocolate bar moulds and leave at cool room temperature (15°C) for 20 minutes, then place in the fridge (5°C) to set completely.

COCOA NIB GIANDUJA

MAKES 49 PIECES 2CM SQUARE

It's hard to believe that something so simple could be so delicous — this will disappear before your eyes if you have a crowd of friends around. Keeps well in the fridge if you can hide some pieces!

ingredients

100g Almond marzipan (minimum 45% almonds) – see recipe p230
75g Hazelnut praline paste – see recipe p231
100g 33% Madagascar Tanariva milk chocolate, small pieces or callets
30g Cocoa nibs (see note)
100g 65% Plantation Alto El Sol Peru dark chocolate, small pieces or callets

method

1. Roll the marzipan into a 15cm square 2mm thick and place into a flexi-silicone or loose-bottom baking tin of at least 15mm depth.
2. Melt the milk chocolate 1½ minutes/50°C/Speed 3 until about three quarters of the chocolate is melted, pausing to scrape down the sides of the TM bowl once, then mix without heat 2 minutes/Speed 3 until completely melted and smooth.
3. Add the praline and cocoa nibs and stir them in thoroughly with the TM spatula.
4. Pour onto the marzipan and wait until the wet shine completely disappears and it has just set.
5. Melt and temper the dark chocolate in the same way as in Step 2, then pour it gently over the milk chocolate layer. For decoration, if desired, it is possible to do some rapid piping in and feathering with a fork if working quickly before the dark chocolate sets.
6. As soon as the chocolate is dry to the touch, mark into pieces with a long knife.
7. Remove from the tin or flexipan before cutting all the way through when completely set.

JANIE'S TIP:

Cocoa nibs are broken pieces of roasted cocoa beans – they add crunch and a lovely, slightly bitter flavour. You can use raw cacao nibs in this recipe with the added benefit of natural enzymes which are a good boost for the immune system.

SARAH BERNHARDT

MAKES 25

Make the raspberry semi-confit for these inventive treats 24 hours ahead.

ingredients

STOCK SYRUP:

700g Granulated sugar
100g Glucose
500g Water

**RASPBERRY SEMI-CONFIT
(OR RASPBERRIES IN SYRUP):**

100g Syrup (above)
100g Frozen raspberries
50g Brandy
10g Raspberry eau de vie
  – optional

LIGHT BUTTER GANACHE:

250g Soft unsalted butter, diced
150g Icing sugar or fondant
  powder
250g 54% dark chocolate or
  375g 33% milk chocolate, small
  pieces or callets

ASSEMBLY:

25 Soft macaroons, flavour of
  your choice – see recipes p198
  and p216

Light butter ganache

88

RASPBERRY SEMI-CONFIT:

1. Cook the stock syrup 30 minutes/Varoma Temperature/Speed 2, replacing the TM Measuring Cup with the internal steaming basket to allow the liquid to reduce.
2. Pour 100g of the hot syrup over the frozen raspberries in a bowl, add the brandy, and add the eau de vie if using.
3. Cover and refrigerate for 24 hours.

LIGHT BUTTER GANACHE:

1. Warm the chocolate 4 minutes/37°C/Speed 3, pausing once to scrape down the sides of the TM bowl.
2. Mix 2½ minutes/Speed 3 without heat until all the chocolate is melted and smooth then pour out into a small jug or bowl and set aside.
3. In the same TM bowl, cream the butter and icing sugar together 4 minutes/Speed 4, pausing once to scrape down.
4. With the TM running at Speed 4, pour the melted chocolate in a steady stream through the hole in the TM lid then mix to an airy but stable consistency (about 30 seconds longer).

ASSEMBLY:

1. Spread a little butter ganache on the top of a macaroon then place a well drained raspberry on top.
2. Pipe the butter ganache in a peak shape over it, using a plain piping nozzle.
3. Repeat with the remaining macaroons.
4. Let set well, then enrobe in tempered dark or milk chocolate and decorate to your choice.

CHOCOLATE LACE BOWLS AND SPHERES

MAKES 4

ingredients

500g 70% Dark chocolate,
   small pieces or callets

Equipment

Polycarbonate mould: semi-sphere
   approx 12cm diameter
Small piping bags
Palette knife

method

1. Place the mould/s in a freezer for 1 hour.
2. Grind the chocolate 10 seconds/Speed 10.
3. Melt 3 minutes/50°C/Speed 3; scrape down the sides of the TM bowl – there should be about 30% to 40% of the chocolate still solid – and immediately continue mixing without heat 3 minutes/Speed 2 or longer until completely smooth and at 32°C (stop your TM and remove lid to check temperature with a probe).
4. Fill the piping bag and remove the mould from the freezer.
5. Wipe any condensation from the inner surface of the mould to prevent sticking and start piping immediately by 'dropping' small, interconnected loops of chocolate. Start from the centre and work outwards right up to the rim. Finish the rim with a solid line of chocolate and scrape the flat surface clean with a palette knife.
6. Refrigerate for 20 minutes or until the chocolate has detached from the mould, then remove the semi-sphere carefully. Pushing on one side should then swivel it out of the mould.
7. Either upturn and use as a serving bowl for dessert items or enclose the dessert items in a sphere for decoration.
   To do this place the top edges of two semi-spheres on a warm flat plate until the full circle of the rim begins to melt, place the dessert inside, then simply place one semi-sphere rim precisely on top of the other.
8. After 5 minutes or when set, food colouring can then be applied with a soft paintbrush or clean buffing cloth.

MILK YORKSHIRE CHOCOLATES

MAKES 750G

The rapeseed oil in this ganache produces a slightly unusual flavour that will have everyone guessing.

ingredients

YORKSHIRE MILK GANACHE:

200g Yorkshire double cream
500g 33% milk chocolate, e.g. Callebaut 823 NV, small pieces or callets
40g Yorkshire unsalted butter
10g Organic cold-pressed rapeseed oil from Collingham, Wetherby
Melted milk chocolate, tempered, for dipping
Transfer sheet or textured sheet

method

GANACHE:

1. Melt the cream, milk chocolate, butter and oil 2½ minutes/50°C/Speed 3, pausing twice to scrape down the sides of the TM bowl.
2. Finish melting 2 minutes/Speed 4 without heat until completely smooth.
3. Pour 1cm deep into a frame or tray and leave to set for 24 hours.
4. When set, coat the top of the ganache with tempered milk chocolate and leave to set again - this will later be turned upside down to become the bottom of your chocolates.
5. Cut into small squares and dip each one into tempered milk chocolate. Place onto a cocoa butter transfer or textured plastic sheet and leave to set.

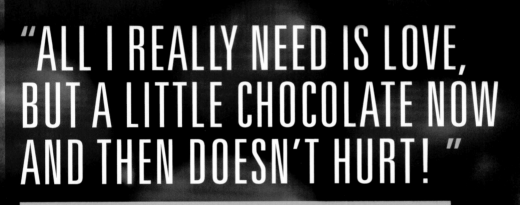

"ALL I REALLY NEED IS LOVE, BUT A LITTLE CHOCOLATE NOW AND THEN DOESN'T HURT!"

LUCY VAN PELT (IN PEANUTS, BY CHARLES M. SCHULZ)

95

NERO DELIGHT

MAKES 40

These little biscuits are wonderful with or without the cocoa nibs, and the coating of dark chocolate on the base is a lovely surprise when you bite into them.

ingredients

150g Granulated sugar
50g Cocoa block (see note)
250g Butter, diced, soft
100g Free-range eggs, weighed
    without shells (about 2 large)
300g Plain flour
1 pinch Ground cinnamon
Cocoa nibs – optional
Apricot jam
Melted tempered dark chocolate
    for dipping

method

1. Preheat the oven to 220°C.
2. Grind sugar to icing sugar 30 seconds/Speed 10. Tip out and set aside.
3. Chop the cocoa block 20 seconds/Speed 10, scrape down the sides of the TM bowl with the spatula, then melt 1½ minutes/50°C/Speed 1, pausing once to scrape down again.
4. Add the sugar and butter, cream well 1 minute/Speed 4 then scrape down again.
5. With the TM running at Speed 3, add the eggs and mix until incorporated. Don't worry if it curdles at this point.
6. Add the cinnamon and flour then fold in 10 seconds/Speed 4 or until mixed well.
7. Pipe the mixture into rosettes (with a star tube) onto silpat mats or silicone sheets, sprinkle with cocoa nibs if using, and bake for 5-7 minutes.
8. Cool on a rack, then turn the biscuits over, brush the flat side with warmed apricot jam and allow to dry.
9. Dip the flat bases into melted chocolate and either place onto transfer sheets or mark as you wish or place onto a silicone sheet and leave until set.

NOTE:

What is cocoa block? After roasting, cocoa beans are ground finely into a cocoa mass or paste. The mass is then melted and becomes liquor. The liquor is cooled and moulded into blocks known as cocoa block or unsweetened baking chocolate or bitter chocolate.

MANCHESTER TART CHOCOLATES

MAKES 36 CHOCOLATES

The Manchester Tart is a traditional pudding mentioned by Mrs Beeton in her famous cookery books and fondly remembered from English school dinners in the 1950s and '60s. This is John Slattery's modern twist, recreating the flavours in a small chocolate — perfect for after dinner.

ingredients

CHOCOLATE SHELLS:

500g 33% milk chocolate, e.g. Callebaut 823 NV, small pieces or callets plus more if needed

WHITE CHOCOLATE CUSTARD GANACHE:

270g White chocolate, e.g. Callebaut W2 NV, small pieces or callets
130g Whipping cream
½ tsp Vanilla paste or 1 tsp real vanilla extract or seeds of ½ vanilla pod
1 tbsp Custard powder
35g Liquid glucose, heated in a pan until hot but not boiling

TO ASSEMBLE:

75g Very good raspberry jam (see excellent TM recipe in 'Demonstrator Delights')
75g Desiccated coconut

method

1. Grate the milk chocolate 10 seconds/Speed 8, then melt 3 minutes/50°C/Speed 3.
2. Scrape down the sides of the TM bowl and mix 3 minutes/Speed 2 without heat. Remove the TM lid – the chocolate should be completely melted and smooth and between 30°C and 31°C on a temperature probe, i.e. tempered.
3. If it's above 31°C, add 30g chocolate and stir again 3 minutes/Speed 2, pausing once to scrape down the sides of the TM bowl with the spatula. Repeat if necessary until tempered.
4. Mould a chocolate case. Allow to set. (Although each empty chocolate case weighs only 7g, remember you will need to temper additional chocolate to allow for filling the moulds, emptying them and working with the chocolate – the excess can be used again another time.)
5. Pipe a generous bulb (2g) of raspberry jam into the base of each set chocolate case.

WHITE CHOCOLATE CUSTARD GANACHE:

1. Melt the chocolate, cream, vanilla and custard powder 4 minutes/37°C/Speed 2, pausing once or twice to scrape down the sides of the TM bowl with the spatula.
2. Remove the TM lid and avoiding the blade unit, add the glucose to the chocolate then stir 2 minutes/Speed 2 without heat until the chocolate is completely melted and smooth. Remove the TM lid and check temperature with a probe – it should be between 29°C to 30°C, i.e. tempered.
3. Pour out into a small bowl and leave to stand (covered) overnight at room temperature.

98

4. Return the ganache to the TM bowl and aerate 30 seconds/Speed 4.
5. Transfer to a piping bag fitted with a 7mm or 8mm plain tube.
6. Pipe the ganache to seal over the jam in the base and fill just over the brim of the chocolate case.
7. Sprinkle with desiccated coconut and allow to set.

JOHN'S NOTE:
These chocolates are best enjoyed fresh, because the ganache filling is exposed (i.e. not sealed in with chocolate to protect it) and the air will dry it out.

SNOBINETTE CHICKS

MAKES 25

These cheeky little chicks are actually tiny iced cakes in chocolate shells called snobinettes.
This perfect butter cream recipe can be used with or without limoncello for icing other cakes too.

ingredients

LIMONCELLO BUTTER CREAM:

200g Granulated sugar
200g Soft butter, diced
30 to 50g Hot water (not boiling)
   from the kettle
Real vanilla extract, to taste
Limoncello liqueur, to taste

ASSEMBLY:

Dark or milk snobinettes (small
   chocolate cups)
Plain vanilla sponge discs (see
   Praline Chocolate Tart recipe p176
Passion fruit syrup
Passion fruit purée
Yellow sugar
Royal icing

method

LIMONCELLO BUTTER CREAM:

1. Grind the sugar to icing sugar 30 seconds/Speed 10.
2. Insert the Butterfly Whisk, add the butter and whisk
    20 seconds/Speed 3, pausing to scrape down the sides of the
    TM bowl as needed.
3. Set the scales to zero and weigh 50g hot water into the
    TM Measuring Cup, then turn to Speed 3 and gradually add
    about one third of the hot water through the hole in the
    TM lid. Pause to scrape down the sides of the TM bowl, then
    repeat, adding just enough of the remaining hot water to
    create a light butter cream.
4. Finish by whisking in the vanilla and/or Limoncello as desired.

ASSEMBLY:

1. Place a small round of vanilla sponge in the bottom of each
    snobinette.
2. Brush with passion fruit syrup and pipe some passion fruit
    purée on top.
3. Pipe butter cream over it in a dome shape.
4. Pipe a small blob of butter cream on top (as the head) and
    sprinkle with dry yellow sugar.
5. Decorate the head of each chick using royal Icing.

100

CHOCOLATE DIPPED
CANDIED FRUIT

SERVES 10 OR MORE

ingredients

500g Caster sugar
500g Honey
750g Water
500g Whole fruit e.g. cherries,
    clementines or sliced fruit e.g.
    pineapple, oranges
200g 75% Tanzanie dark chocolate,
    small pieces or callets

method

1. Boil the sugar, honey and water in a heavy saucepan, stirring constantly, until it reaches 112°C on a temperature probe.
2. Add the small fruit whole or large fruit sliced and simmer until the fruit is translucent.
3. Drain and cool on a rack above a tray (to catch the drips) then leave to dry overnight.
4. Melt the chocolate 4 minutes/37°C/Speed 3, scrape down the sides of the TM bowl – about half to three quarters should be melted, then continue mixing at Speed 3 without heat until completely smooth.
5. Use skewers or toothpicks to dip the fruit in the melted chocolate and place on a silpat mat or silicone sheet to cool completely.
6. Fill a piping bag with the remaining melted chocolate and decorate as desired. Leave to set for at least 1 hour or until the chocolate has fully contracted and squeezed any excess juice from the fruit.

CHOCOLATE TRUFFLES

MAKES 25-30 TRUFFLES

A small box or gift bag of home-made truffles makes a lovely gift for any occasion.

ingredients

200g Whipping cream
200g 70% dark chocolate, e.g.
   Callebaut 70-30-38 NV, small pieces
   or callets
75g Unsalted butter, diced
150g Melted tempered chocolate,
   for rolling
30 to 50g Cocoa powder, for rolling

method

1. Heat cream, chocolate and butter 3 minutes/50°C/Speed 2.
2. Scrape down the sides of the TM bowl and stir without heat at Speed 2 to melt the remaining bits of chocolate – it should end up completely smooth.
3. Pour into a bowl, cool for about 1 hour to room temperature, then cover and refrigerate overnight until set.
4. Roll into small balls about 2cm diameter, place on a tray and return to the fridge.
5. Wearing plastic disposable gloves, dip each truffle in melted chocolate and roll in the palms of your hands to create a slightly ridged coating on the truffle, then place on a silicone sheet to set.
6. Roll in cocoa powder to finish.

JANIE'S TIP:

You can use any firm chocolate ganache recipe to make truffles, with or without coating them in tempered chocolate.

CHOCOLATE DISCS WITH
FRUIT AND SEEDS

MAKES 250 TO 300G

ingredients

200g Callebaut 811 NV, 54% dark
  chocolate, small pieces or callets
Mixed seeds of choice – e.g.
  pumpkin, sunflower, flax, sesame
Dried Fruit of choice – e.g. raisins,
  goji berries, cranberries, sultanas

method

1. Grind the chocolate 10 seconds/Speed 8.
2. Melt the chocolate 4 minutes/37°C/Speed 2; scrape down
   the sides of the TM bowl and continue mixing without heat
   2 minutes/Speed 2 or until it reads 32°C (stop your TM and
   remove lid to check temperature with a probe).
3. Pipe the chocolate in discs about 3cm in diameter on
   silicone paper.
4. Lift the paper and shake gently to flatten the piped discs then
   sprinkle immediately with the mixed seeds and fruit.
5. Leave to set and serve when required.

P.C.P.
— PINE NUT, CRANBERRY AND PRALINE

MAKES 20 SLICES

Such a simple way to create a delicious sweet treat. Perfect as a dessert, or enrobe small pieces to serve as an after dinner chocolate.

ingredients

200g 33% milk chocolate, e.g. Callebaut 823 NV, small pieces or callets
400g Praline paste – see recipe p231
100g Feuilletine – see recipe p226
35g Toasted pine nuts
25g Dried cranberries and/or dried cherries
100g Milk, dark and/or white chocolate, tempered, for decoration

method

1. Melt the 200g milk chocolate 2 minutes/50°C/Speed 3, scrape down the sides of the TM bowl and finish the melting 2 minutes/Speed 3 without heat. The chocolate should be completely melted and smooth.
2. Add the praline paste, feuilletine, pine nuts and cranberries. Stir well 20 seconds/Speed 2/Reverse Blade Direction or until all evenly mixed – you may need to stir with the TM spatula through the hole in the TM lid.
3. Leave in a cool place to firm slightly.
4. Deposit onto cling film and roll up to form two 'sausages' each 20-23cm in length.
5. Tightly roll each 'sausage' in a sushi mat and secure with elastic bands – this will create a ridged surface once it's set.
6. Refrigerate for at least 2 hours or until completely firm.
7. Unroll, discard the cling film, and if desired, coat with tempered milk chocolate using a knife or brush to form a 'tree bark' effect.
8. Serve cut in slices – delicious!

JOHN'S NOTES:

To create a contrast, use dark chocolate to coat the roll, or white chocolate can look particularly festive. And of course the inclusions can be swapped to form different initials… the possibilities are limited only by your imagination and good taste!

W.P.C. Walnut, Praline, Cashew
R.B.P. Raisin, Brazil, Praline
G.P.H. Ginger, Praline, Hazelnut

This recipe can alternatively be formed in a baking tray; when set, cut into small squares and fully enrobe them in chocolate.

DESSERTS

BAILEYS WHITE CHOCOLATE MOUSSE

SERVES 8 TO 10 AS A DESSERT OR SERVES 24 AS A PRE-DESSERT OR AS ONE COMPONENT ON A DESSERT SELECTION PLATE

This versatile delicious mousse will make your guests swoon with delight! Serve on its own or as a layer in a cake.

ingredients

300g Full-fat milk
45g Custard powder
30g Vanilla sugar
250g White chocolate, e.g. Callebaut W2 NV, small pieces or callets
30g Cocoa butter, e.g. Mycryo ®
45g Baileys Irish Cream liqueur
400g Whipping cream

method

1. Cook the milk, custard powder and vanilla sugar 6 minutes/90°C/Speed 4.
2. Add the chocolate, cocoa butter and liqueur, then stir 2 minutes/Speed 4 or until all the chocolate and cocoa butter are melted and the mixture is smooth.
3. Pour out into a large bowl and leave to cool.
4. Meanwhile, insert the Butterfly Whisk into a clean TM bowl and whip the cream at Speed 3 until JUST softly whipped.
5. When the custard mixture is 29°C to 30°C on a temperature probe, fold in the whipped cream.

TO SERVE:

1. Pipe into glasses, use as a layer in a cake, or use as the main filling in a Yule chocolate log.

NOTE:

This recipe can also be used with other flavours. Instead of Baileys, try coffee and Tia Maria, coffee and rum, raspberry with a raspberry liqueur, or orange purée with Grand Marnier. Use your imagination and be creative!

CHESTNUT CHOCOLATE TORTE

SERVES 16

This delicious torte is definitely fast and easy with your Thermomix — it can be eaten warm or cold, or made the day before you need it (if you can keep everyone away from it so it can last until the next day).

ingredients

4 Free-range large egg whites
80g Granulated sugar
350g Chestnut purée – see tip below
140g Full-fat milk
90g Brown sugar
250g Unsalted butter, diced, soft
240g Peru Piura Porcelana, 75% dark chocolate

method

1. Preheat the oven to 180°C.
2. Grease and line a 23cm round tin.
3. Insert the Butterfly Whisk in a clean grease-free TM bowl and whisk the egg whites and granulated sugar 5 minutes/37°C//Speed 3 until it forms a stiff glossy meringue. Tip out and set aside (or use your other TM bowl for the next step).
4. Heat the chestnut purée, milk, brown sugar, butter and chocolate 5 minutes/50°C/Speed 3, pausing once to scrape down the sides of the TM bowl with the spatula.
5. Scrape down again and mix 2 minutes/Speed 4 without heat until it is a smooth homogeneous mixture and the chocolate is all melted, then pour out into a large bowl.
6. Fold one third of the meringue into the chocolate mixture to slacken it, then gently fold in the rest.
7. Pour into the prepared tin and bake for about 30 minutes, removing from the oven when set (there should be a slight movement in the middle).
8. Allow to cool completely before serving.

JANIE'S TIP:

To make your own chestnut purée, substitute 350g cooked chestnuts; after setting aside the meringue, blend the chestnuts with the milk 40 seconds/Speed 4 until smooth, stopping once or twice to scrape down the sides of the TM bowl with the spatula, then add the brown sugar, butter and chocolate and continue with Step 4.

115

SMOOTH CHOCOLATE PANCAKES SERVED WITH CHOCOLATE ICE CREAM AND WARM CHERRIES TOPPED WITH CHOCOLATE SAUCE

MAKES ENOUGH FOR 4 SERVINGS

These thin pancakes are similar to crêpes and are a lovely dessert for a family meal or gathering of friends. To make the pancakes ahead of time, layer them with greaseproof paper and wrap the stack — they can be frozen like this too. Try serving them with Mark Tilling's chocolate sorbet.

ingredients

SMOOTH CHOCOLATE PANCAKES:

2 Free-range large eggs
50g Caster sugar
600g Semi-skimmed milk
220g Plain flour
20g Cocoa powder, e.g. Cacao Barry
   Extra Brute
30g Butter, very soft
Oil, for frying

CHOCOLATE SAUCE:

150g Double cream
150g Callebaut 811 NV, 54%
   dark chocolate

TO SERVE:

Chocolate ice cream or Chocolate
   sorbet – see recipe p142
150g Fresh cherries warmed in a light
   sugar syrup flavoured with a
   splash of Kirsch

method

SMOOTH CHOCOLATE PANCAKES:

1. Blend the eggs, sugar, milk, flour, cocoa powder and butter 30 seconds/Speed 8.
2. Heat a small amount of oil in a frying pan over moderate heat, pour in sufficient batter to just cover the base of the pan, allow to set then turn over and cook for a few seconds on the bottom side until done.
3. Turn out onto a piece of greaseproof or silicone paper – pile up the pancakes as you continue cooking them.

CHOCOLATE SAUCE:

1. Melt the cream and chocolate 3 minutes/50°C/Speed 3, scrape down the sides of the TM bowl with the spatula.
2. Mix 3 minutes/Speed 3 without heat until completely melted and smooth.

TO SERVE:

1. Once the pancakes are cool, fill each one with two small scoops of chocolate ice cream or sorbet.
2. Wrap to create a parcel, place on a plate then spoon some of the Kirsch cherries over the pancake, followed by the hot chocolate sauce. Serve immediately.

MILK CHOCOLATE SWIRL FILLED WITH JAVA ORIGIN CHOCOLATE MOUSSE

SERVES 4

ingredients

CHOCOLATE SWIRL CYLINDERS:

250g 33% milk chocolate, e.g.
   Callebaut 823 NV, small pieces or
   callets

JAVA ORIGIN CHOCOLATE MOUSSE:

200g Full-fat milk
35g Custard powder
20g Granulated sugar
20g Cocoa butter, e.g. Callebaut
   Mycryo ®
250g Callebaut origins Java
   milk chocolate, small pieces or
   callets
400g Whipping cream or
   double cream

TO SERVE:

4 Chocolate swirl cylinders
Chocolate sponge – see recipe p146
2 tsp Kirsch per serving
300g Java Origin Chocolate Mousse
Red berries, physalis and a white
   chocolate trellis per serving to
   decorate

method

MILK CHOCOLATE SWIRL:

1. Pour the melted tempered milk chocolate onto a frozen marble slab and use an offset palette knife to smooth it into a thin oblong about 24x35cm.
2. As soon as you see that the chocolate is firming up but not yet set (which happens within seconds), work quickly and use the edge of your palette knife to cut this oblong into four equal strips. Lift them off the slab by scraping underneath them with your palette knife, then quickly and gently roll into cylinders of about 6cm in diameter, allowing a piece of 4cm to stick out (see photo). Leave the cylinders to set.

JAVA ORIGIN CHOCOLATE MOUSSE:

1. Cook the milk, custard powder, sugar and cocoa butter 5 minutes/90°C/ Speed 4.
2. Add the chocolate and stir at Speed 3 until melted and completely smooth, pausing to scrape down the sides of the TM bowl once or twice.
3. Pour out into a large bowl and leave the mixture to cool for about 15 minutes.
4. Insert the Butterfly Whisk in a clean TM bowl, add the cream and whip at Speed 3 JUST until softly whipped.
5. When the custard is 29°C to 30°C on a temperature probe, fold in the whipped cream. The mousse is now ready to be piped.

TO SERVE:

1. Place a chocolate swirl on a plate. Cut round discs from the sponge the diameter of the cylinder and soak them with the kirsch.
2. Place one disc in the bottom of the cylinder and fill the cylinder half-way with the mousse. Place another disc of sponge onto the mousse and finish with a nice swirl of the mousse to the top of the cylinder.
3. Decorate with berries and physalis and place a white chocolate trellis on top.

CHOCOLATE AND TOFFOC SOUFFLE

MAKES 10

What better combination than chocolate with a smooth caramel toffee. Toffoc is a delicious toffee vodka from Wales which manages to release a smooth flavour with a kick! This can be a gluten-free dessert if you use corn flour.

ingredients

PASTRY CREAM:

80g 70% dark chocolate, e.g. Callebaut 70-30-38 NV, small pieces or callets
4 Free-range large egg yolks
50g Granulated sugar
30g Plain flour or corn flour
250g Full-fat milk
1 Vanilla pod, seeds only

MERINGUE:

8 Free-range large egg whites
150g Caster sugar
40g Toffoc Vodka

method

PASTRY CREAM:

1. Chop the chocolate 8 seconds/Speed 7 and set aside for later.
2. Cook the egg yolks, sugar, flour, milk and vanilla seeds 6 minutes/90°C/Speed 4.
3. Pour into a large clean bowl, place cling film over the surface to prevent a skin forming, and then cool to room temperature.

MERINGUE:

1. Insert the Butterfly Whisk into a clean grease-free TM bowl and whisk the egg whites and sugar 8 minutes/Speed 3 – you will have a stiff and glossy meringue.
2. Add the liqueur and mix 5 seconds/Speed 3.
3. Add one quarter of the meringue to the cooled pastry cream and mix until smooth.
4. Gently fold in the remaining meringue and the reserved chopped chocolate.
5. Fill buttered and floured ramekins to the top and place on a baking tray.
6. Bake in a hot oven at 210°C for 7-10 minutes until well risen and golden on top.
7. On removal from the oven dust with icing sugar and serve immediately.

JOHN'S NOTE:

Whilst I think the Toffoc is ideal in this recipe, the alcohol can be changed to suit your palate, Grand Marnier or Cointreau being more traditional.

JANIE'S TIP:

If you have two TM bowls, leave the pastry cream to cool in your first TM bowl and make the meringue in your second TM bowl. In this case, mix the cooled pastry cream at Speed 5 for a few seconds until smooth before pouring out into a bowl and folding in the meringue.

ROULADE GRIOTTINE

SERVES 8-10

ingredients

CHOCOLATE SPONGE:

130g Free-range egg whites
65g Caster sugar
130g Free-range egg yolks
40g Plain flour
20g Cocoa powder

DARK CHOCOLATE MOUSSE:

150g Callebaut 811 NV, 54%
   dark chocolate, small pieces or
   callets
300g Whipping cream

TO FINISH:

1 small jar Griottine cherries

method

CHOCOLATE SPONGE:

1. Sieve the cocoa powder and flour by Turbo pulsing a few times. Tip out and set aside in a large bowl.
2. Insert the Butterfly Whisk into a clean grease-free TM bowl and whisk the egg whites with the sugar 7 minutes/Speed 3 into a glossy meringue.
3. Add the egg yolks and mix 10 seconds/Speed 3.
4. Place a jam funnel into the hole in the TM lid and with the TM running at Speed 2½, gradually add the flour/cocoa mix.
5. Spread onto a lined baking tray approximately 20x30cm and bake at 190°C for about 12 minutes.
6. Leave in the tin, covered with a sheet of greaseproof paper and a damp tea towel for 8 hours or overnight.

DARK CHOCOLATE MOUSSE:

1. Melt the dark chocolate 2 minutes/50°C/Speed 3, scrape down the sides of the TM bowl, then mix without heat 2 minutes/Speed 3 until completely smooth and pour into a large bowl.
2. Insert the Butterfly Whisk into a clean TM bowl and whip the cream at Speed 3 JUST until lightly whipped.
3. Fold half the cream into the chocolate, then fold in the remainder.
4. Turn the chocolate sponge onto a sheet of greaseproof paper dusted with icing sugar or granulated sugar and peel away the paper from the bottom of the cake.
5. When the cake is cool, spread half the chocolate mousse over the sponge, sprinkle the griottine cherries on top and roll into a roulade using the paper to help.
6. Place seam side down on a serving dish and cover with the remaining chocolate mousse.
7. Finish with decorations of your choice and/or a few more griottine cherries.

JANIE'S TIP:

Griottines are cherries macerated in eau de vie or kirsch.

122

CUP DENMARK

SERVES 6

ingredients

CHOCOLATE SAUCE:

300g 54% dark chocolate, e.g.
   Callebaut 811 NV, small pieces or
   callets
160g Water
80g Whipping cream
1 Vanilla pod, seeds only
20g Unsalted butter

ASSEMBLY:

Vanilla ice cream – see excellent
   recipe in *'Fast and Easy Cooking'*
Whipped cream
Toasted flaked almonds

method

CHOCOLATE SAUCE:

1. Chop the chocolate 20 seconds/Speed 8 then scrape down the sides of the TM bowl with the spatula.
2. Add remaining sauce ingredients and heat 7 minutes/ 60°C/Speed 3, pausing to scrape down the sides of the TM bowl twice.
3. Serve hot.

ASSEMBLY:

1. Place the ice cream in a pre-chilled cup or glass.
2. Press a hollow into the ice cream with the back of a spoon.
3. Decorate the edge with whipped cream and sprinkle with almonds.
4. Serve with a jug of hot chocolate sauce – to be poured into the hollow of the ice cream at the table.

124

"STRENGTH IS THE CAPACITY TO BREAK A CHOCOLATE BAR INTO FOUR PIECES WITH YOUR BARE HANDS - AND THEN EAT JUST ONE OF THE PIECES."

JUDITH VIORST

BAKED LEMON AND WHITE CHOCOLATE CHEESECAKE

MAKES 8 GENEROUS PORTIONS

The base of this cheesecake adds a wonderful flavour and texture contrast to the creamy filling.

ingredients

BASE:

300g Ginger biscuits or Speculaas biscuits
150g Butter, diced
100g Dried fruit, e.g. raisins, apricots and cherries
50g Flaked almonds

CHEESECAKE FILLING:

300g Mascarpone cheese
200g Ricotta cheese
200g Single cream
6 Free-range large eggs
2 organic lemons, grated zest and 60g of the freshly-squeezed juice
200g white chocolate, small pieces or callets

TOPPING:

Fruit glaze
Fresh raspberries – optional
Lemon zest – optional

TO SERVE:

Red fruit coulis
White chocolate decorations
Raspberries

method

BASE:

1. Chop the dried fruit by Turbo pulsing briefly a few times. Tip out and set aside.
2. Grind the biscuits and butter 1 minute/100°C/Speed 4.
3. Mix in the chopped fruit and flaked almonds 1 minute/ Speed 3/Reverse Blade Direction or until well mixed. Press into the bottom of a lined 24cm spring form tin. Place in the fridge to harden.

CHEESECAKE FILLING:

1. Mix the cheeses, cream, eggs, lemon juice (add extra to make the juice up to 60g if necessary) and zest 30 seconds/ Speed 8.
2. Stir in the white chocolate and pour the mixture on top of the chilled biscuit base – use a spatula to carefully make sure the white chocolate is evenly spread out.
3. Bake at 110°C (fan) for about 1 hour 15 minutes. Take out of the oven and allow to cool then refrigerate for at least 6 hours.

Fruit chopped in seconds

Cheesecake base

TOPPING:

1. Take out of the spring form tin and brush the top with a fruit glaze – melted smooth jam works well. Decorate with fresh raspberries, lemon or lime zest.

TO SERVE:

1. Serve a wedge with a red fruit coulis on the plate and a white chocolate decoration plus raspberries on top.

CARAMEL MOUSSE

MAKES 8 DESSERTS PLUS ABOUT 20 EXTRA BISCUITS

This delicate mousse is a real treat for your tastebuds! Serve it on these lovely white chocolate sablé biscuits as Ruth does, or just on its own — it's delicious both ways. The biscuit recipe makes more than you need, but the extras will find an appreciative reception I'm sure.

ingredients

CARAMEL MOUSSE:

Fills 8 silicone mini-charlotte or large muffin moulds
2 Leaves gelatine
430g Double cream, divided 100g and 330g
200g Callebaut caramel flavoured chocolate (or 33% Milk chocolate if you haven't got caramel chocolate), small pieces or callets

BISCUIT BASE:

Makes about 30 biscuits 7cm diameter
150g Icing sugar
70g Ground almonds
250g Unsalted butter, diced, soft
1 Small free-range egg
400g Plain flour
20g Corn flour
1 good pinch Sea salt
130g Callebaut W2 NV white chocolate, small pieces or callets

method

CARAMEL MOUSSE:

1. Soak the gelatine leaves in cold water for 5 minutes.
2. Heat the 100g cream 2 minutes/70°C/Speed 2.
3. Avoiding the TM blades, add the drained gelatine and mix 1 minute/Speed 3 to dissolve.
4. Add the chocolate and mix at Speed 3 until fully melted and smooth, pausing to scrape down the sides of the TM bowl twice. If it doesn't completely melt, warm it 20 seconds/50°C/Speed 3 at a time until melted and smooth. Transfer to a large bowl to cool to about 30°C while you whip the cream.
5. Insert the Butterfly Whisk into a clean TM bowl and whip the 330g cream until JUST softly whipped.
6. Fold one third of the whipped cream into the chocolate then fold in the rest.
7. Fill 8 silicone mini-Charlotte moulds (e.g. Demarle Flexipan with 8 Charlotte indents) or silicone mould/s of your choice.
8. Place in the freezer or fridge and allow to set before popping them out. If frozen solid, they will need about 1½ hours (out of the moulds) at room temperature to defrost before serving.

SABLE BISCUIT BASE:

1. Mix all the biscuit ingredients 30 seconds/Speed 5.
2. Scrape down the sides of the TM bowl and mix again at Speed 5 for a few seconds.
3. Roll into a log, wrap with greaseproof paper or cling film and chill in the fridge for at least 1 hour.
4. Slice or roll out and cut to shape, then bake at 180°C for about 15 minutes until pale gold in colour.

TO SERVE:

1. Sit the caramel mousses on the sablé biscuits and garnish as you wish.

JANIE'S TIPS:

1. If you need to make some icing sugar, grind granulated sugar 30 seconds/Speed 10.

2. For ground almonds, grind whole almonds about 12 seconds/Speed 10 until fine.

3. If you don't want to bake all the biscuits at once, you can keep the extra dough in the fridge for up to 2 weeks. Then you can produce beautiful biscuits fresh from the oven at a moment's notice! The biscuit dough can also be frozen for up to 3 months.

BITTER CHOCOLATE MOUSSE

SERVES 2

This dessert is very simple to make and is lovely for a special dinner for two. It can also be doubled or tripled for a dinner party.

ingredients

100g Amedei Venezuela Porcelana dark chocolate 70%, small pieces or callets
1 pinch Freshly ground nutmeg
2 Free-range large eggs, separated
2 heaped tsp Whipped cream, to garnish
40g Grated dark chocolate and/or chopped toasted hazelnuts
2 Stemmed wine glasses or ramekins

method

1. Melt the chocolate with the nutmeg 2 minutes/50°C/ Speed 3 until fully melted and smooth, pausing once or twice to scrape down the sides of the TM bowl.
2. While mixing at Speed 3, add the egg yolks through the hole in the TM lid and mix in thoroughly – it will thicken immediately. Transfer to a large bowl.
3. Insert the Butterfly Whisk into a clean grease-free TM bowl (you could use your second TM bowl), add the egg whites and whisk 3 minutes/Speed 3 to soft peak stage.
4. Stir one quarter of the egg whites into the chocolate mixture, repeat with another quarter, then gently fold in the remainder.
5. Spoon the mixture into the glasses, cover each with cling film and chill until firm, about 2 hours.
6. Top with whipped cream and some grated chocolate or chopped nuts.

DOUBLE CHOCOLATE BAKED CHEESECAKE

MAKES 8 INDIVIDUAL 7.5CM ROUND CHEESECAKES

This recipe, inspired by a cheesecake John Slattery tasted in New York, gives you a failsafe delicious-to-eat confection that never fails to please.

ingredients

BASE:

130g Digestive biscuits, broken
25g Golden syrup
25g Unsalted butter, diced

FILLING:

130g White chocolate, small pieces
    or callets
70g Dark chocolate 70%, small pieces
    or callets
330g Full-fat cream cheese
85g Caster sugar
20g Corn flour
1 Free-range large egg
170g Whipping cream

method

BASE:

1. Mix the digestive pieces, golden syrup and butter 2 minutes/100°C/Speed 4.
2. Place 25g of the base mix into each 7.5cm diameter ring (place the rings on silicone sheets on baking trays). Press the crumb mix down firmly.

FILLING:

1. Melt the white chocolate 3 minutes/50°C/Speed 2 until completely melted and smooth, pausing once or twice to scrape down the sides of the TM bowl, then pour into a large bowl.
2. Melt the dark chocolate 2½ minutes/50°C/Speed 3 until completely melted and smooth, pausing once or twice to scrape down the sides of the TM bowl, then pour into another large bowl.
3. Blend the cheese, sugar, corn flour, egg and cream 30 seconds/Speed 8.
4. Scrape down the TM bowl with the spatula and blend again 10 seconds/Speed 8.
5. Pour half the filling mix into the white chocolate and mix thoroughly.
6. Pour the remaining filling mix into the dark chocolate and mix thoroughly until no streaks remain.

ASSEMBLY:

1. Spoon or pipe equal amounts of each flavour side by side into the rings.
2. With a circular motion using a skewer, create a marble effect on the top.
3. Bake at 160°C for 35-40 minutes.
4. Check the centre of the cheesecakes – they should reach 72°C on a temperature probe.
5. Once baked, this cheesecake can be cooled and frozen if required.

JANIE'S TIP:

This cheesecake is also wonderful unbaked – just chill at least 3 hours until set and enjoy its creamy texture!

ORANGE AND GINGER
CHOCOLATE STEAMED SPONGE SERVED WITH DRAMBUIE CHOCOLATE SAUCE

MAKES 8 SMALL PUDDINGS

ingredients

ORANGE AND GINGER CHOCOLATE STEAMED SPONGE:

1 Organic orange, thin peelings of the skin only
120g Caster sugar
120g Butter
100g Plain flour
1 tsp Baking powder
20g Cocoa powder, e.g. Cacao Barry Extra Brute, minimum 20% cocoa butter
2 Large free-range eggs
30g Milk
50g Crystallised ginger

DRAMBUIE CHOCOLATE SAUCE:

150g Callebaut 811 NV, 54% dark chocolate
150g Double cream
30g Drambuie, or to taste

method

ORANGE AND GINGER CHOCOLATE STEAMED SPONGE:

1. Butter 8 dariole moulds and dredge them with plain flour.
2. Grind the orange peelings and sugar 30 seconds/Speed 10 until fine.
3. Add remaining ingredients and mix 20 seconds/Speed 5.
4. Fill the dariole moulds three-quarters full, cover each mould with buttered greaseproof paper and secure with an elastic band, then place into the Varoma.
5. Add 1 litre of water to the TM bowl then steam the puddings 40 minutes/Varoma Temperature/Speed 1 (or 45 minutes if the water was very cold to start).
6. Unmould the hot puddings and serve immediately with Drambuie chocolate sauce.

DRAMBUIE CHOCOLATE SAUCE:

1. Melt all sauce ingredients 4 minutes/50°C/Speed 3.
2. Scrape down the sides of the TM bowl and mix again 2 minutes/Speed 3 without heat.
3. Taste and add more Drambuie if desired.

JANIE'S TIP:

I like to serve this with a dollop of softly whipped cream to balance the sweetness of the pudding and sauce.

136

137

BELGIAN WAFFLES

BELGIAN WAFFLES

MAKES ABOUT 20 LARGE WAFFLES

ingredients

BATTER:

100g Butter, diced
250g Plain white flour
25g Icing sugar
½ tsp Fine sea salt
10g Fresh yeast or 1 tsp instant yeast
250g Full-fat milk
2 Large free-range eggs
250g Lukewarm water

WAFFLES:

Vegetable oil

TO SERVE:

Icing sugar
Ice cream, fresh fruit, fruit coulis,
   chocolate or butterscotch sauce/s,
   as desired

method

BATTER:

1. Melt the butter 1 minute/100°C/Speed 4.
2. Add remaining ingredients except the water and blend
   1 minute/37°C/Speed 8.
3. Add the water and mix 20 seconds/Speed 6.
4. Place the batter in a warm place until doubled in volume.

WAFFLES:

1. Use an electric waffle maker. The waffle plates have to be
   very hot. Oil the plates with some vegetable oil or coconut oil.
2. Pour a ladle of batter onto each plate and close the waffle
   maker. Cook for 3-5 minutes until golden brown.

TO SERVE:

1. Dust with icing sugar, serve with ice cream, fruit, fruit coulis
   and/or a chocolate or sticky toffee sauce – see wonderful
   recipe in *'Demonstrator Delights'*.

JANIE'S TIP:

If you don't want to cook all the waffles at once, the mixture
keeps well in the fridge for up to 2 days – stir it down once or
twice a day.

CHOCOLATE SORBET

MAKES ABOUT 1.2 LITRES

Sorbets are delicious and refreshing icy desserts and this one is no exception. Using traditional methods, they take all day to make, but this version is much faster with your Thermomix.

ingredients

260g Granulated sugar
65g Cocoa powder, 20% cocoa butter minimum
100g Dark chocolate, small pieces or callets
50g Liquid glucose
100g Water
600g Ice cubes

method

1. Grind the sugar, cocoa and chocolate 30 seconds/ Speed 10 then scrape down the lid and sides of the TM bowl with the spatula.
2. Heat the glucose and water in a small pan on the hob until bubbling.
3. Avoiding the TM blade unit, add the hot glucose then mix 30 seconds/Speed 4.
4. Scrape down the sides of the TM bowl, add the ice and blend 1 minute/Speed 10 until smooth, pausing halfway to scrape down the sides of the TM bowl again.
5. Freeze in a shallow box for 2 hours or longer until solid.

JANIE'S TIP:

If desired, you can cut the frozen sorbet into 3cm chunks and churn:
- For the whole amount, churn at Speed 9 while stirring with the TM spatula through the hole in the TM lid.
- For just one or two portion/s, turn gradually up to Speed 5 until smooth and creamy – no need to churn with the TM spatula.

JANIE'S VARIATION:

Add 100g hazelnuts or almonds at Step 1 and grind 1 minute/ Speed 10 with the sugar, cocoa and chocolate.

CHOCOLATE AND PEAR
BREAD AND BUTTER PUDDING

SERVES 6

Chocolate and pear have often been 'dessert partners'. This recipe creates a hot pudding where the intense chocolate notes are balanced by soft, smooth fruit.

ingredients

200g 70% dark chocolate, e.g.
  Callebaut 70-30-38 NV, small pieces
  or callets
75g Butter, diced
110g Caster sugar
420g Whipping cream
3 Free-range large eggs
2 pinches Ground cinnamon
200g Day-old white bread,
  weighed after crusts removed
2 Pears, peeled, poached and sliced
  into wedges (tinned pears can be
  used)

NOTE:

I prefer this pudding served hot accompanied by a poached pear and a pool of fresh cream (as illustrated). However, if you assemble and bake it in a shallow dish and allow it to cool completely, the pudding can be cut into small cubes or triangles and served as a canapé dessert or as part of a trio of mini chocolate desserts served together.

method

1. Melt the chocolate, butter, sugar and cream 5 minutes/50°C/Speed 2, pausing once to scrape down the sides of the TM bowl.
2. Add the eggs and cinnamon, blend 30 seconds/Speed 6.
3. Cut the bread into small squares or triangles and dip each piece into the mix, allowing a few seconds to absorb the custard.
4. Arrange alternately with the drained sliced pears in buttered individual ramekins or 1 large oven-proof dish, and pour any remaining custard over the top.
5. Bake at 180°C for 30-40 minutes for the large dish or 20-25 minutes for individual dishes (it is ready when it springs back when you press the middle, like a sponge cake).
6. Serve hot or cold.

JOHN'S NOTE:

While I prefer to use plain white bread in this recipe because it is less sweet, you can use brioche or panettone to create a softer, sweeter eat.

144

JAVA ORIGIN
MILK CHOCOLATE AND RUM GATEAU

SERVES 4

ingredients

DARK CHOCOLATE SPONGE:

4 Free-range large eggs
100g Caster sugar
1 pinch Sea salt
75g Self-raising flour
50g Cocoa powder, e.g. Van Houten
Butter to grease the mould

GATEAU:

4 Square pieces of dark chocolate
    sponge 3mm thick
Dark rum, as required
250g Java Origin Milk Chocolate
    Mousse – see recipe p146
White and dark chocolate vermicelli
Some red berries, star fruit and
    chocolate curls to decorate

method

DARK CHOCOLATE SPONGE:

1. Sieve the flour and cocoa powder by Turbo pulsing 4 or 5 times, then tip out and set aside.
2. Insert the Butterfly Whisk, add the eggs, sugar and salt and whisk 6 minutes/37°C/Speed 3.
3. Insert a jam funnel into the hole in the TM lid, turn to Speed 2½, and gradually add the flour/cocoa mix.
4. Scrape down the sides of the TM bowl with the spatula and mix again a few seconds/Speed 2½.
5. Pour into a butter-greased baking tray and bake for about 20 minutes at 200°C.
6. Cool in the tray for 20 minutes then turn over onto a clean wire rack and allow to cool completely before cutting – you will need 4 squares 10x10cm.
7. Left over chocolate sponge can be frozen and used at a later date.

GATEAU:

1. Use a loose-bottom square tin about 10x10x10cm. Line the tin with cling film, place in the bottom of the tin a square of chocolate sponge then sprinkle dark rum over it to taste. Pipe some mousse onto the sponge and repeat the layers three more times. Finish the top by smoothing the mousse then place in the freezer.
2. After 4 hours take the gateau out of the freezer and with a blow torch heat the sides of the tin just enough to loosen the cake. Take the cake out of the tin and allow it to defrost in the fridge.
3. Coat alternate sides with the white and dark vermicelli. Decorate the top with chocolate curls, the star fruit and some berries. When serving the gateau use a warm knife (dip it into hot water and dry it) to cut it into portions; dip and wipe the knife before each cut.

CHOCOLATE NEMESIS

SERVES 10

This is John's take on what has become a classic, and this wonderful dessert, served hot with the contrast of a cold smooth ice cream, is a delicious pudding.

ingredients

5 Free-range large eggs
280g Caster sugar
120g Water
330g Dark chocolate 70% or above, small pieces or callets
220g Unsalted butter, diced

TO SERVE:

Vanilla ice cream

method

1. Insert the Butterfly Whisk and whisk the eggs, sugar and water 10 minutes/70°C/Speed 4.
2. Remove the Butterfly Whisk, set a dish on top of the TM lid, press the scales to zero and weigh into it the butter. Repeat with the chocolate.
3. Set the TM to Speed 3 and gradually add the diced butter.
4. Keep mixing at Speed 3 and add one third of the chocolate at a time through the hole in the TM lid, continuing to mix after each addition until you can hear that it's melted and smooth.
5. When fully melted, pour the mix into ramekins and bake at 150°C for 45-50 minutes.
6. Serve hot with vanilla ice cream.

JOHN'S NOTE:

In the original famous recipe from The River Café this dessert is baked in a water bath, but John has discovered that following the above method gives a more open texture to the cake which he thinks is preferable when served warm. Serve with a shot of chocolate sauce for added luxury if you wish.

CHARLOTTE VANILLA CHOCOLATE

SERVES 8-10

ingredients

CHOCOLATE SPONGE:

40g Plain flour
20g Cocoa powder
130g Free-range egg whites
65g Caster sugar
130g Free-range egg yolks

VANILLA MOUSSE:

60g Caster sugar
50g Free-range egg yolks
250g Full-fat milk
½ Vanilla pod, seeds only
2½ leaves Gelatine
250g Whipping cream

CHOCOLATE MOUSSE:

130g Callebaut Origins Java
   milk chocolate, small pieces or
   callets
130g Callebaut Origins Madagascar
   dark chocolate, small pieces or
   callets
500g Whipping cream

method

CHOCOLATE SPONGE:

1. Sieve the flour and cocoa powder by Turbo pulsing a few times, tip out and set aside.
2. Insert the Butterfly Whisk into a clean grease-free TM bowl then whisk the egg whites and sugar 6 minutes/Speed 3 to form a stiff meringue.
3. Add the egg yolks and mix 10 seconds/Speed 3.
4. Insert a jam funnel into the hole in the TM lid, set the TM to Speed 2½ and add in the flour/cocoa mix.
5. Scrape down the sides of the TM bowl with the spatula and mix again a few seconds at Speed 2½ then spread onto a large lined oven tray and bake at 190°C for about 12 minutes.
6. Cut a 4cm strip of cake and use to line the inside (i.e. the sides) of a 20cm diameter by 4.5cm high cake ring or loose-bottom cake tin. Cut two discs to fit inside the ring.

VANILLA MOUSSE:

1. Soak the gelatine leaves in cold water for 5 minutes.
2. Meanwhile, cook the sugar, egg yolks, milk and vanilla seeds 5 minutes/80°C/Speed 4.
3. Add the drained gelatine leaves and mix 20 seconds/Speed 4. Pour into a large bowl and leave to cool to body temperature.
4. Insert the Butterfly Whisk into a clean TM bowl and whip 750g cream at Speed 3 until JUST softly whipped – watch it carefully and stop as soon as it looks softly whipped on top because it will be more whipped underneath.
5. Fold one third of the whipped cream into the cooled custard mix and set the rest aside for the chocolate mousse later.
6. Place one sponge disc in the base of the ring and add the vanilla mousse. Place the second sponge disc on top of the vanilla mousse.

CHOCOLATE MOUSSE:

1. Melt the milk and dark chocolates together in a clean TM bowl 3 minutes/50°C/Speed 3, scrape down the sides of the TM bowl with the spatula, then continue mixing 2 minutes/Speed 3 without heat to finish melting the chocolate.
2. Pour the smooth melted chocolate into a large bowl and fold in the reserved lightly whipped cream.
3. Finish by piping the chocolate mousse over the top decoratively.

151

POACHED SPICED PEAR WITH VANILLA PARFAIT AND BITTER CHOCOLATE MOUSSE

POACHED SPICED PEAR WITH VANILLA PARFAIT AND BITTER CHOCOLATE MOUSSE

SERVES 4

Make the poached pears two days in advance so the red wine can penetrate the core of the pears. Make and freeze the parfait and make the chocolate mousse one day in advance, and the red wine jelly if using. Then it's easy to serve this dessert for a dinner party as all you need to do on the day is assemble it!

ingredients

POACHED PEARS:

4 Small pears
250g Red wine
¼ tsp Chilli flakes
1 small Cinnamon stick
1 Star anise
3 Cloves
10 Black peppercorns
50g Granulated sugar

PARFAIT:

4 Free-range large egg yolks
75g Caster sugar
1 Vanilla pod, seeds only
220g Whipping cream

CHOCOLATE MOUSSE:

50g Caster sugar
4 Free-range large egg whites
100g 70% dark chocolate, e.g.
    Callebaut 70-30-38 NV, small pieces
    or callets
4 Free-range large egg yolks

TO SERVE:

4 Squares 6x6cm milk chocolate
4 Squares 6x6cm dark chocolate
4 Chocolate sticks of about
    12cm long
Chocolate, melted, as required
Chopped hazelnuts, as required

method

POACHED PEARS:

1. Make these two days in advance so that the red wine can penetrate the core of the pear. Peel the pears, leaving the stem intact. Infuse the red wine with the spices and sugar and bring to the boil in a pan. Add and submerge the pears, then simmer gently until they are cooked. Cool in the pan, then refrigerate the pears in the red wine syrup.

PARFAIT:

1. Insert the Butterfly Whisk and whisk the egg yolks, sugar and vanilla seeds 8 minutes/60°C/Speed 3.
2. Continue whisking 20 minutes/Speed 3/Measuring Cup OFF. Tip out and set aside.
3. Whip the cream at Speed 3 until JUST softly whipped. Fold gently into the egg mix.
4. Pour the parfait mixture into a bowl or shallow box and freeze overnight.

CHOCOLATE MOUSSE:

1. Insert the Butterfly Whisk into a clean, grease-free TM bowl, add the egg whites and sugar, then whisk 7 minutes/Speed 3 – you will have a thick glossy meringue.
2. Add the egg yolks through the hole in the TM lid, mix 10 seconds/Speed 3 then pour out into a large bowl and set aside (or leave in this TM bowl and use your second TM bowl for melting the chocolate).
3. Melt the chocolate in a clean TM bowl 2 minutes/50°C/Speed 2, pausing once or twice to scrape down the sides of the TM bowl.

4. Continue mixing at Speed 3 until completely melted and smooth.
5. Fold one third of the meringue into the melted chocolate, then fold in the rest until no streaks remain.
6. Spoon or pour into small glasses and chill.

TO SERVE:

1. Take the squares of milk and dark chocolate and carefully cut out a little hole in the top right-hand corner (using a hot knife). Take the chocolate sticks and dip the ends into the melted chocolate and then into the chopped hazelnuts.
2. Place a spicy pear in the middle of an oblong plate. Place a scoop of vanilla parfait between a milk and a dark chocolate square, then press slightly so that the parfait is sandwiched between the two chocolate squares.
3. Push a chocolate stick through the holes to connect the two chocolate squares, not piercing the parfait. Place a glass with the bitter chocolate mousse on the right.

NOTE:

This recipe can also be served with a Red Wine Jelly made from the strained pear liquid. Simply soak 4 gelatine leaves in cold water for 5 minutes while you bring the pear liquid to the boil, add the drained softened gelatine and stir into the pear liquid until dissolved. Pour into a tray, cool 20 minutes then set in the fridge. Serve by cutting into small squares of 0.5cm, scattering four or five around each pear.

RASPBERRY CARDINAL

SERVES 10

This certainly gets a big "ooh!" at a dinner party and this easily created dessert has a taste to match its good looks.

ingredients

SWEET PASTRY:

(makes enough for 2x23cm
tart shells):

350g Plain flour
100g Caster sugar
250g Unsalted butter, diced, cold
2 Free-range medium eggs
Melted dark chocolate or cocoa
   butter, for brushing
Fresh raspberries

GANACHE:

25g Liquid glucose
250g Whipping cream
200g 70% dark chocolate, e.g.
   Callebaut 70-30-38 NV, small pieces
   or callets
80g Unsalted butter, diced

DECORATION:

Fresh raspberries
Chocolate ruffles

method

SWEET PASTRY:

1. Turbo pulse the flour, sugar and butter until it looks like fine crumbs.
2. Add the eggs and mix at Speed 6 until JUST clinging together in clumps.
3. Pat into a flat disc, wrap and refrigerate for at least 30 minutes.
4. Roll out half of the pastry using a minimum of flour and line a greased 23cm loose-bottom flan tin. Freeze the remaining pastry to use another time.
5. Place the unbaked tart shell into the refrigerator to rest for at least 30 minutes to help prevent shrinkage during baking.
6. Prick the base with a fork then bake blind at 180°C for 10-15 minutes.
7. Remove baking beans and parchment paper; return the tart shell to the oven until pale gold in colour and baked through.
8. Once the pastry case is cool, brush the inside with melted

chocolate or cocoa butter to prevent it becoming soggy when filled.

9. Cover the base with raspberries.

GANACHE:

1. Heat the glucose in a small pan on the hob then set aside.
2. Heat the cream, chocolate and butter 2 minutes/37°C/Speed 3.
3. Scrape down the sides of the TM bowl and add the warm glucose.

4. Mix 2 minutes/Speed 3 without heat until all the chocolate is melted and completely smooth.
5. Pour into the pastry shell, cover with raspberries and allow to set.
6. Decorate with fresh raspberries and chocolate ruffles then chill.
7. Remove from fridge 1 hour before serving.

PASTRY

CHOCOLATE **TART**

CHOCOLATE **TART**

A rich decadent confection which will impress everyone, perfect for dinner parties and special occasions. Decorate to your own taste with fruit, chocolate curls or biscuits — or enjoy on its own as a luxurious chocolate treat.

ingredients

PASTRY:

A good sweet shortcrust pastry to line or block into individual foil cases or to line a 28cm loose-bottom tart tin (see recipe for Raspberry Cardinal on p156).

FILLING:

220g Whipping cream
200g Full-fat milk
5 Free-range large egg yolks
70g Granulated sugar
130g 70% dark chocolate, e.g.
    Callebaut 70-30-38 NV, small pieces
    or callets

method

FILLING:

1. Cook the cream, milk, egg yolks and sugar 8 minutes/80°C/ Speed 3.
2. Add the chocolate and stir 2 minutes/Speed 3 to melt — it should be completely smooth.
3. Transfer to a piping bag, tie the top and leave until room temperature, or cool and refrigerate in a sealed container until required.
4. Lightly part-bake the pastry case/s at 200°C until pale gold, about 7-8 minutes for tartlets or about 9-12 minutes for the large tart.
5. Pipe or spoon the filling (with a slight dome) into the cooled pastry case/s.
6. Bake tartlets at 170°C for 20-25 minutes until set then allow to cool completely before serving. For a 28cm tart, bake 30-35 minutes.
7. Add chocolate decorations if desired.

NOTE:

Release your creative side — for instance, John makes a delicious Chocolate Orange Tart with the addition of a tangy orange curd in the base before the chocolate filling is piped in. Orange curd is wonderful made in your Thermomix — see the Lemon Curd recipe in 'Fast and Easy Cooking' for a method.

You could also try replacing the dark chocolate with white or caramel chocolate.

BRITTANY WITH
CHOCOLATE CREAM

MAKES 8 TO 10 PLUS 20 EXTRA BISCUITS

ingredients

CHOCOLATE CREAM:

130g Double cream
120g Milk
25g Granulated sugar
50g Free-range egg yolks, about
    3 large
150g Callebaut 811 NV, 54% dark
    chocolate, small pieces or callets

BISCUIT BASE:

130g Caster sugar
150g Unsalted butter, diced
1 tsp Fleur de Sel sea salt from
    Brittany
50g Free-range egg yolks
200g Plain flour
1 tsp Baking powder

TO SERVE:

Fresh raspberries

method

CHOCOLATE CREAM:

1. Cook the cream, milk, sugar and yolks 5 minutes/90°C/
    Speed 4.
2. Add the chocolate, mix about 30 seconds at Speed 3 until
    completely smooth then pour out into a bowl, cover, and
    leave to cool overnight.
3. Return the mixture to the TM bowl, gradually increase to
    Speed 5 and mix until completely smooth then transfer to a
    piping bag.

BISCUIT BASE:

1. Mix all the biscuit ingredients 20 seconds/Speed 5.
2. Scrape down the sides of the TM bowl with the spatula, mix
    again 10 seconds/Speed 5, shape dough into a log, wrap and
    chill for 1 hour in the fridge.
3. Roll out to about 2-3 mm thickness or slice into rounds.
4. Bake at 180°C for about 10-15 minutes or until golden.
5. If baking as a slab, when it comes out of the oven, cut with a
    round cutter or cut into squares and cool.
6. Pipe a mound of chocolate cream into the centre of each
    biscuit, surround with raspberries then garnish with popping
    candy or crispy pearls.

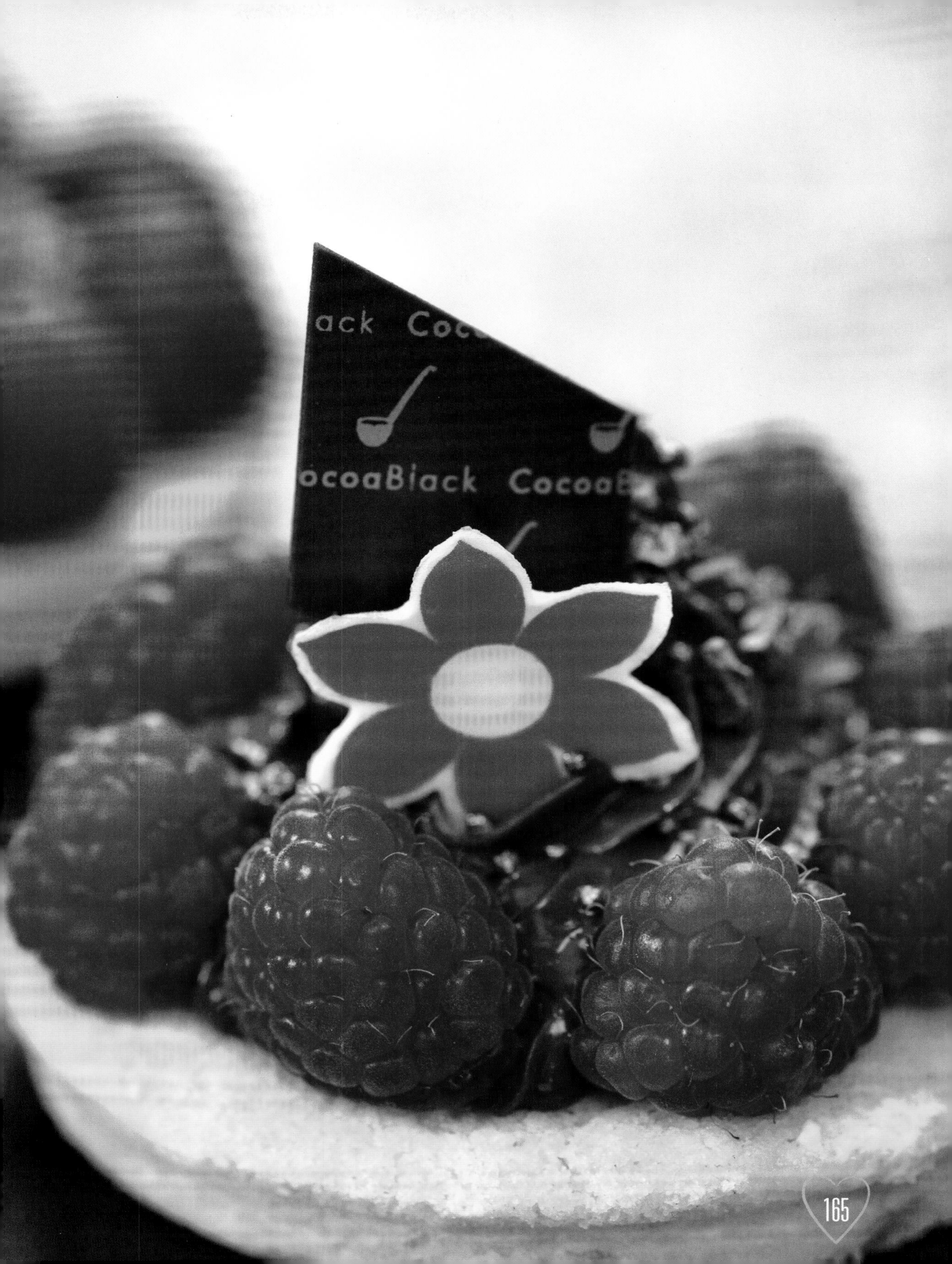
ack Coc
ocoaBlack CocoaB

CHOCOLATE ECLAIRS

CHOCOLATE ECLAIRS

MAKES 24

If you've never made your own éclairs before now, you're really in for a treat - nothing beats home-made for freshness and flavour, and all three components are easy with your Thermomix.

CHOCOLATE PASTRY CREAM – CREME PATISSIERE

ingredients

40g Free-range egg yolks (2 large)
50g Granulated sugar
10g Plain flour
10g Corn flour
250g Full-fat milk
10g Unsalted butter
75g Callebaut 811 NV, 54% dark
   chocolate, small pieces or callets

method

1. Cook all ingredients except the chocolate 7 minutes/90°C/Speed 3.
2. Add the chocolate and stir 3 minutes/Speed 3 or until fully melted.
3. Pour out into a bowl or onto a tray (or leave in TM bowl). Cover immediately and leave to cool. Chill in fridge if not using straight away.
4. When cool, return to TM bowl and gradually turn up to Speed 5 until totally smooth again, then transfer to a piping bag.

CHOUX PASTRY

ingredients

140g Strong flour
10g Cocoa powder, e.g. Cacao Barry
  Extra Brute
100g Butter, diced
250g Water
200g Free-range eggs, weighed
  without shells, about 4 large

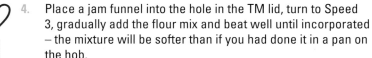

method

1. Preheat the oven to 215°C.
2. In a clean and dry TM bowl, sieve the flour and cocoa powder by Turbo pulsing a few times. Tip out and set aside.
3. Heat the butter and water 5 minutes/100°C/Speed 1, making sure the butter has melted.
4. Place a jam funnel into the hole in the TM lid, turn to Speed 3, gradually add the flour mix and beat well until incorporated – the mixture will be softer than if you had done it in a pan on the hob.
5. Remove the TM bowl from the machine, take off the lid and allow the paste to cool to body temperature.
6. Add the eggs through the hole in the TM lid while mixing at Speed 5 then continue to mix 30 seconds/Speed 5 – the mixture should then fall from a spoon on a count of 5.
7. If the mixture is still too stiff, add a little more beaten egg – the quantity of eggs depends on the strength of the flour: the stronger the flour, the more egg is required.
8. To make éclairs pipe out the pastry to 10cm long with a 1¼ cm plain nozzle onto a buttered and floured tray or silpat mat or demarle flexipan mat.
9. Bake in the preheated oven for about 15 minutes until brown and set.
10. Immediately on removing from the oven, cut a slit into the side of the choux to allow steam to escape.

CHOCOLATE GLAZE FOR ECLAIRS

ingredients

150g Callebaut 811 NV, 54% dark
  chocolate
150g Double cream

method

1. Heat the chocolate and cream 1½ minutes/50°C/Speed 2 then stir without heat 2 minutes/ Speed 2 or longer until melted and smooth.

ASSEMBLY OF ECLAIRS:

1. Pipe the pastry cream into the choux bun.
2. Dip the top of the éclair into the chocolate glaze.
3. Enjoy!

JANIE'S TIP:

Lovely served with a dollop of softly whipped cream.

DARK CHOCOLATE TART
INFUSED WITH COFFEE

MAKES 10 BANQUETTE-MOULDED (BOAT-SHAPED) TARTS

ingredients

SWEET PASTRY:

170g Plain flour
25g Cocoa powder, e.g. Cacao Barry Extra Brute, minimum 20% cocoa butter
50g Caster sugar
100g Salted butter, diced, very cold
1 Free-range large egg

DARK CHOCOLATE AND COFFEE FILLING:

200g Whipping cream
2 tsp Granular instant coffee
200g Callebaut 811 NV, 54% dark chocolate, small pieces or callets

DECORATION:

100g Callebaut 811 NV, 54% dark chocolate, melted and tempered
10g Popping candy

method

SWEET PASTRY:

1. Sieve the flour and cocoa powder together by Turbo pulsing a few times.
2. Add the butter and sugar, Turbo pulse in short bursts until fine crumbs form.

3. Add the egg and Turbo pulse in short bursts JUST until clinging together.
4. Press into desired tartlet cases and chill in a fridge for 1 hour to prevent shrinkage during baking.
5. Bake blind at 180°C for 10-15 minutes, then remove baking beans and paper and return to the oven for a few minutes until pastry is fully baked – watch it carefully and remove when done. Cool in the tins on a rack.

DARK CHOCOLATE AND COFFEE FILLING:

1. Heat the cream and instant coffee 3 minutes/50°C/Speed 3.
2. Add the chocolate and stir to a smooth cream 3-4 minutes at Speed 3 without heat.
3. Set aside for 10 minutes to cool a little then pour into the baked pastry cases, cool at room temperature for 45 minutes then refrigerate for 2 hours.

DECORATION:

1. When you're ready to make the decorations, warm the chocolate in a clean TM bowl 2 minutes/37°C/Speed 2, scrape down the sides of the TM bowl, then finish melting 3 minutes/Speed 2.
2. Decorate with a piped lattice of melted and tempered dark chocolate sprinkled with popping candy.

"ANYTHING IS GOOD IF IT'S MADE OF CHOCOLATE."

JO BRAND

CHOCOLATE PECAN PIE

MAKES 8-10 INDIVIDUAL 10CM PECAN PIES PLUS EXTRA FILLING

It's true that most things taste better with chocolate, and in the case of this pecan pie doubly so, as John Slattery has incorporated chocolate into both the pastry and the delicious filling.

ingredients

CHOCOLATE PASTRY:

180g Plain flour
25g Cocoa powder
50g Caster sugar
130g Butter, diced, very cold
2 Free-range medium egg yolks
30g Water, chilled

CHOCOLATE PECAN FILLING:

350g Caster sugar
300g Real maple syrup or
   golden syrup
100g Unsalted butter, diced
85g Cocoa powder
6 Free-range large eggs
1½ tsp Real vanilla extract or
   1 tsp vanilla paste
400g Pecan nuts
Pecan halves for decoration
   (3 halves for each pie)
Apricot jam glaze, to finish

method

CHOCOLATE PASTRY:

1. Sieve the flour and cocoa powder by Turbo pulsing a few times.
2. Add the sugar and butter, then Turbo pulse until fine crumbs form.
3. Add the egg yolks and water and Turbo pulse in short bursts JUST until the pastry starts clinging together.
4. Tip out, press into foil cases or lined tins (John uses 10cm tin foil cases with a fluted crimp) and refrigerate for at least 30 minutes before adding the filling. This will help prevent shrinkage of the pastry when the tarts are baking.

CHOCOLATE PECAN FILLING:

1. Heat the sugar, syrup and butter 5 minutes/50°C/ Speed 3.
2. Add the cocoa, eggs and vanilla. Mix 15 seconds/ Speed 4 then scrape down the sides of the TM bowl with the spatula.

Chocolate pastry in 6 seconds

3. Add and chop the pecans 10 seconds/Speed 3½ then pour out into a jug or bowl.
4. Set one of the pastry cases onto a plate on the TM lid, set the scales to zero and weigh in 70g of the filling. Repeat with each of the other pastry cases.
5. Decorate the top of each pie with three pecan halves.
6. Bake at 190°C for 20 minutes.
7. Glaze when cool by brushing with warmed apricot jam to seal the tarts.

JOHN'S NOTE:

The filling can be stored in a sealed container in the refrigerator for up to 2 weeks. Fresh tarts can be baked each day from this recipe (stir the filling well before use).

PRALINE CHOCOLATE TART

PRALINE CHOCOLATE TART

SERVES 6

ingredients

SABLE PASTRY:

200g Plain flour
80g Icing sugar
20g Ground almonds
1 pinch Fine sea salt
120g Butter, diced, very cold
1 Free-range large egg
Real vanilla extract, to taste

VANILLA SPONGE SHEET:

500g Free-range eggs, weighed
    without shells, about 10 large
250g Caster sugar
160g Plain flour
50g Corn flour

FRANGELICO SYRUP:

100g Caster sugar
75g Water
40g Frangelico liqueur

**PRALINE MILK
CHOCOLATE GANACHE:**

200g 33% Milk chocolate, small
    pieces or callets
60g 54% Dark chocolate, small pieces
    or callets
220g Whipping cream
110g Praline paste – see recipe p231

method

SABLE PASTRY:

1. Preheat the oven to 180°C.
2. Turbo pulse the flour,
   sugar, almonds, salt and
   butter until sandy.
3. Add the egg and vanilla
   then Turbo pulse in short
   bursts JUST until clinging
   together, tip out, wrap and
   chill 30 minutes.
4. Roll out on a lightly floured
   board and cut to fit six tins
   10cm diameter each.
5. Blind bake for 15 minutes,
   then remove baking
   parchment and baking
   beans and finish baking
   until pastry is pale gold and
   cooked through.

VANILLA SPONGE SHEET:

1. Insert the Butterfly Whisk,
   whisk the eggs and sugar
   10 minutes/37°C/Speed 3.
2. Set a bowl on the TM lid,
   press scales to zero and
   weigh in the flours.
3. Insert a jam funnel into the
   hole in the TM lid, turn to
   Speed 2½ then gradually
   add the flours.
4. Spread evenly on a
   40x60cm baking sheet.
5. Bake at 200°C for 6-8
   minutes.

FRANGELICO SYRUP:

1. Heat the sugar and
   water 5 minutes/Varoma
   Temperature/Speed 1.
2. Add the Frangelico and stir
   5 seconds/Speed 3.
   Set aside to cool.

**PRALINE MILK
CHOCOLATE GANACHE:**

1. Melt the chocolate and
   cream 4 minutes/50°C/
   Speed 2 – about half
   should be melted by now.
2. Scrape down the sides
   of the TM bowl with the
   spatula then mix without
   heat 3 minutes/Speed
   3 until all melted and
   smooth.
3. Add the praline paste and
   mix well at Speed 3.

ASSEMBLY:

1. Place a disc of sponge
   sheet on the base of the
   tartlet and brush it with
   Frangelico syrup.
2. Pour the ganache into the
   prepared tartlets and leave
   to set.
3. Decorate to your choice or
   leave plain.

MILLEFEUILLE CHOCOLAT

SERVES 8-10

ingredients

PUFF PASTRY:

500g Puff pastry – use a classic puff pastry or make the excellent recipe for Rough Puff Pastry in *'Fast and Easy Cooking'*

PASTRY CREAM CHOCOLATE:

500g Full-fat milk
10g Unsalted butter
75g Free-range eggs, weighed without shells
100g Granulated sugar
15g Corn flour
30g Plain flour
75g Callebaut 811 NV, 54% dark chocolate, small pieces or callets
Icing sugar to decorate – optional
Cocoa powder to decorate – optional

method

PUFF PASTRY:

1. Roll out the pastry on a silpat mat or silicone sheet to a 30cm square. Leave to rest while you heat the oven.
2. Bake in a hot oven to start (200°C) for 18-20 minutes, then turn down to 160°C for approximately 40 minutes. The pastry should be dry and crisp.
3. Leave to cool and gently cut into three strips approximately 10cm wide.

PASTRY CREAM CHOCOLATE:

1. Cook milk, butter, eggs, sugar and flours 8 minutes/90°C/Speed 4.
2. Add the chocolate and stir to melt 3 minutes/Speed 3 without heat, then leave to cool on a tray covered with cling film.
3. Return the pastry cream to the TM bowl, gradually turn up to Speed 5 and mix until smooth again.
4. Spread half the pastry cream on top of the first strip of pastry, add the next strip of pastry, the second portion of pastry cream then finally the last pastry strip. Place in the fridge for 1 hour before decorating as you wish.

CHOCOLATE ECLAIRS

CHOCOLATE ECLAIRS

MAKES 20

ingredients

CHOCOLATE PASTRY CREAM:

500g Full-fat milk
10g Butter
75g Free-range eggs, weighed
    without shells
100g Caster sugar
15g Corn flour
30g Plain flour
75g Callebaut 811 NV, 54%
    dark chocolate, small pieces or
    callets

CHOUX PASTRY:

150g Plain flour
1 tsp Fine sea salt
½ tsp Caster sugar
250g Water
100g Unsalted butter, diced
250g Free-range eggs, weighed
    without shells
1 Egg, beaten (egg wash)

GLAZE:

100g Callebaut 811 NV, 54%
    dark chocolate, small pieces or
    callets
100g Bakers chocolate, small pieces
    or callets – see note below
75g Stock syrup at room temperature
    – see recipe p88
120g Full-fat milk

method

CHOCOLATE PASTRY CREAM:

1. Cook all ingredients except
   the chocolate
   9 minutes/90°C/Speed 3.
2. Add the chocolate and stir
   3 minutes/Speed 3 or until
   fully melted.
3. Pour out into a bowl or onto
   a tray (or leave in TM bowl).
   Cover immediately and
   leave to cool. Chill in fridge
   if not using straight away.
4. When cold, return to
   TM bowl and gradually turn
   up to Speed 5 until totally
   smooth again, then transfer
   to a piping bag.

CHOUX PASTRY:

1. Preheat the oven to 190°C.
2. In a clean and dry TM bowl,
   sieve the flour by Turbo
   pulsing a few times. Tip out
   and set aside.
3. Heat the butter and water
   5 minutes/100°C/Speed 1,
   making sure the butter has
   melted.
4. Place a jam funnel into the
   hole in the TM lid, turn to
   Speed 3, gradually add the
   flour and beat well until
   incorporated – the mixture

will be softer than if you
had done it in a pan on the
stove.
5. Remove the TM bowl from
   the machine, take off the lid
   and allow the paste to cool
   to body temperature.
6. Add the eggs through the
   hole in the TM lid while
   mixing at Speed 5 then
   continue to mix 30 seconds/
   Speed 5 – the mixture
   should then fall from a
   spoon on a count of 5.
7. If the mixture is still too stiff,
   add a little more beaten
   egg – the quantity of eggs
   depends on the strength
   of the flour: the stronger
   the flour, the more egg is
   required.
8. Pipe long éclair shapes
   onto a lined baking tray
   using a plain nozzle.
9. Apply egg wash and, using
   a fork, mark the top gently.
   This will prevent the éclair
   from losing its shape.
10. Bake in an oven at 190°C for
    10 minutes and then lower
    the temperature to 160°C
    for a further 10 minutes (or
    more if necessary).

GLAZE:

1. Heat the chocolates, stock syrup and milk 2 minutes/50°C/ Speed 2, scrape down the sides of the TM bowl, then stir without heat 2 minutes/ Speed 2 or longer until melted and smooth.
2. Leave to cool in a shallow bowl until slightly thickened so it will coat the top of the éclair.

TO FINISH:

1. When the éclairs are cold, cut down one side lengthways and fill with the chocolate pastry cream.
2. Glaze the top and decorate with chocolate.

THIERRY'S NOTE:

Bakers chocolate is made with some vegetable oil and we use this for our éclair topping as this allows the glaze to stay a little soft. If you wish to use chocolate made only with cocoa butter, use 90g chocolate and 10g sunflower oil instead of the bakers chocolate.

185

"I WOULD GIVE UP CHOCOLATE BUT I'M NO QUITTER."

ANON

TEATIME TREATS

HAZELNUT BROWNIES

MAKES ABOUT 20 BROWNIES

ingredients

50g Hazelnuts plus extra for topping
150g 54% dark chocolate, e.g.
   Callebaut 811 NV, small pieces or
   callets
50g Praline paste – see recipe p231
250g Butter, cubed, soft
4 Free-range large eggs
150g Plain flour
Chocolate bake-stable drops
   or callets
Hazelnut pieces
Icing sugar, to finish – optional

method

1. Grind the 50g hazelnuts 15 seconds/Speed 8.
2. Add the chocolate and praline paste and heat 5 minutes/
    37°C/Speed 2 until the chocolate is melted, pausing to scrape
    down the sides of the TM bowl once or twice.
3. Add butter, eggs and flour then mix 30 seconds/Speed 5.
4. Spoon or pipe the mixture into silicone moulds of your choice
    or into a fairy cake tin lined with paper cases. Sprinkle some
    small chocolate bake-stable drops and crushed hazelnut
    pieces on top.
5. Bake for about 15 minutes at 180°C – they should still be a
    little soft in the middle when you take them out of the oven.

190

GARDEN MINT TRUFFLE
HOT CHOCOLATE

SERVES 2

ingredients

1 full sprig (about 20g) of fresh garden mint

100g Fresh full-fat milk (i.e. not UHT)

10g Fresh double cream (i.e. not UHT)

10g Honey

100g Venezuela Araguani 72% dark chocolate, small pieces or callets

10g Madagascar Tanariva 33% milk chocolate, small pieces or callets

method

1. Set a mug on top of the TM lid and weigh in the milk, then add the mint leaves and push them under the surface of the milk. Leave the milk and mint in the fridge to infuse overnight.

2. Pour the milk through a sieve into the TM bowl, discarding the mint.

3. Avoiding the TM blades, add the cream and honey and heat 2 minutes/90°C/Speed 2.

4. Add the chocolate and mix 1 minute/80°C/Speed 4 or until melted and smooth.

5. Serve in two small (espresso) cups with additional fresh cream, sliced strawberries or a leaf of mint to garnish as desired.

VARIATION:

Make Cinnamon Hot Chocolate by using a crushed stick of cinnamon instead of mint.

MILLIONAIRE'S
SHORTBREAD

MAKES 36 PIECES ABOUT
5CM X 3CM

The caramel has a beautiful flavour when cooked in the Thermomix, and you don't have to stand and stir it.

ingredients

BASE:

150g Granulated sugar
450g Self-raising or plain flour
300g Butter, diced

CARAMEL:

100g Butter
75g Granulated sugar
40g Golden syrup
200g Condensed milk

CHOCOLATE:

200g Callebaut 823 NV, 33% milk chocolate, or 811 NV dark chocolate, small pieces or callets

method

BASE:

1. Grind the sugar 5 seconds/ Speed 10.
2. Add the flour and butter and mix 30 seconds/50°C/ Speed 4.
3. Pat firmly into your baking tray or frame about 30x22cm.
4. Bake at 160°C for about 15-20 minutes, it should be light golden brown.

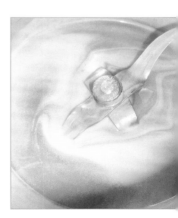

Caramel

CARAMEL:

1. Cook the butter, sugar, golden syrup and condensed milk 25 minutes/Varoma Temperature/ Speed 2, replacing the TM Measuring Cup with the internal steaming basket.
2. Stop the TM, remove the lid and check with a temperature probe – it's done when it reaches 116°C. You may need to cook it quite a lot longer (5 minutes/Varoma Temperature/Speed 2 each time until done) if the air is humid or it's raining.
3. Pour the caramel onto the shortbread base, spread it out evenly then leave to cool and set.

CHOCOLATE:

1. Wash and dry the TM bowl. Add the chocolate pieces. Chop a few seconds on Speed 6 then scrape down the sides of the TM bowl.
2. Melt 2 minutes/50°C/Speed 1 then stir 3 minutes/ Speed 3 without heat until the chocolate is completely melted and smooth.
3. Pour onto the cooled caramel, spread thinly to cover it and leave about 20 minutes – when partially set, mark into pieces.
4. Cut all the way through when quite cold.

CHEWY CHOCOLATE OVERLOAD COOKIES

MAKES APPROX 30 BISCUITS

For the full impact of chewy chocolate sensation, eat and enjoy these biscuits while still warm!

ingredients

120g Unsalted butter, diced, soft
250g Dark brown sugar
1 tsp Real vanilla extract
1 Free-range large egg
150g Plain flour
35g Self-raising flour
1 tsp Bicarbonate of soda
35g Cocoa powder, e.g. Cacao Barry
    Extra Brute
100g Raisins
60g Dark chocolate chunks or callets
60g Milk chocolate chunks or callets
60g White chocolate chunks or callets
100g Callebaut 811 NV, 54% dark
    chocolate callets or chips

method

1. Preheat the oven to 180°C.
2. Mix the butter, sugar, vanilla, egg, flours, bicarb and cocoa 30 seconds/Speed 5.
3. Add the raisins and chocolate chunks then stir to mix 20 seconds/Speed 3/Reverse Blade Direction.

4. Form into small rounds about the size of a walnut and place onto greased baking trays or silpat mats about 4cm apart. Flatten slightly.
5. Bake in the oven for 10 minutes. Cool for 5 minutes and then transfer to a cooling rack.

MACAROONS

MAKES 50 TO 60 MACAROONS

Macaroons are a lovely treat any time, and you'll have a real feeling of accomplishment making them yourself!

ingredients

MACAROONS:

120g Blanched almonds
220g Icing sugar
100g Free-range egg whites
 (3 to 4 large)
¼ tsp Cream of tartar
25g Caster sugar
Flavouring or food colouring –
 optional

CHOCOLATE BUTTER CREAM:

150g White or dark chocolate,
 small pieces or callets
100g Butter, diced, soft
20g Icing sugar
Flavouring, e.g. a liqueur of choice –
 optional

method

MACAROONS:

1. Grind the almonds 12 seconds/Speed 10 until fine then scrape down the sides of the TM bowl with the spatula.
2. Add the icing sugar and grind again 10 seconds/Speed 10 then tip out and set aside.
3. Insert the Butterfly Whisk into a clean grease-free TM bowl (you can use your second TM bowl for this if you have one), whisk the egg whites, cream of tartar and caster sugar 5 minutes/Speed 3 to a stiff glossy meringue, then transfer to a large bowl.
4. Stir the flavouring and/or food colouring if using into the meringue then very gently fold in a quarter of the almond/ sugar powder at a time until you have a smooth and shiny mixture.
5. Pipe 2cm diameter macaroons onto a silicone mat and allow to dry and form a slight crust for 30 minutes.
6. Bake at 160°C (without fan) for about 10 minutes.
7. Remove from oven and remove the silicone sheet from the baking tray – set aside to cool. Use a clean palette knife to lift one from the silicone sheet – if they are baked enough, it will come off quite easily. If it sticks, return the macaroons to the oven and bake a little longer. With macaroons, you are aiming for the perfect combination of dry outside and soft chewy inside.
8. Store in airtight containers until needed.

CHOCOLATE BUTTER CREAM:

1. Melt the chocolate 2 minutes/50°C/Speed 3, pausing to scrape down the sides of the TM bowl once or twice with the spatula, then mix 3 minutes/Speed 3 without heat until completely melted and smooth. Transfer to a shallow dish to

cool while you do the next step.

2. Insert the Butterfly Whisk and cream the soft butter and icing sugar 2 minutes/Speed 3.

3. Add flavouring if using, followed by the melted chocolate, mix 20 seconds/Speed 3, then scrape down the sides of the TM bowl with the spatula and mix again a few seconds.

4. Pipe or spoon a little of the butter cream onto a macaroon, place another macaroon on top and lightly press down; repeat until all the macaroons are paired.

DIRK'S NOTE:

This easy chocolate butter cream can also be used as a filling for a gateau or Swiss roll.

JANIE'S TIP:

Try filling your macaroons with other butter creams and ganaches too – there are several recipes in this book you could use (John Huber's raspberry ganache is one of my favourites – see recipe p82) and with all these recipes as patterns/templates, all you need to do is use your creativity to create new flavours.

CHOCOLATE SPREAD

MAKES 475G

ingredients

200g Whipping cream
100g 33% Milk chocolate, small
   pieces or callets
75g 54% Dark chocolate, small pieces
   or callets
100g Unsalted butter, diced, soft

method

1. Heat all ingredients 5 minutes/50°C/Speed 3 or until melted and smooth, pausing to scrape down the sides of the TM bowl twice.
2. Place into a container in the refrigerator and leave to set overnight.

FLORENTINES

12 INDIVIDUALS

These classic biscuits are wonderfully crisp and nutty. Serve with a cup of tea or coffee and only leave them out if you don't mind them disappearing, because you'll find that everyone nibbles as they walk by.

ingredients

250g Double cream
250g Granulated sugar
75g Salted butter, diced
40g Liquid glucose
95g Honey
250g Flaked almonds
100g Sultanas or raisins
Dark, milk or white chocolate (melted and tempered) - optional

method

1. Cook the cream, sugar, butter, glucose and honey 15 minutes/ Varoma Temperature/Speed 2, replacing the TM Measuring Cup with the internal steaming basket placed on the TM lid.

2. Add the almonds and raisins, stir 10 seconds/Speed 2/ Reverse Blade Direction then scoop into a silicone sheet with 9cm round cookie indents, or place heaped teaspoons onto silicone sheets and flatten the mounds with the back of the spoon so there is about 10cm between them as they will spread more when cooking.

3. Bake at 180ºC until golden brown. This will take about 10-15 minutes and you'll know when they're done because the caramel will be bubbling and the edges will be turning light brown.

4. Allow to cool completely then pop out of the indents or lift off the silicone sheets. Store in an airtight tin with baking paper between the layers.

RUTH'S NOTE:

Dip the bottom of each biscuit in melted tempered chocolate if you wish.

202

CHOCOLATE PECAN BROWNIES

MAKES 35

It's a real treat — delicious soft gooey brownies. Simple to make, they are a hit time after time, and this basic brownie recipe can be very versatile. Try substituting your favourite nuts for the pecans — walnuts, macadamias, brazils and even chopped peanuts all work well.

ingredients

200g 70% dark chocolate, e.g. Callebaut 70-30-38 NV, small pieces or callets
25g Strong coffee, freshly made
120g Unsalted butter, diced, soft
220g Caster sugar
1 tsp Vanilla paste or real vanilla extract
2 Free-range medium eggs
1 Free-range egg yolk
130g Plain flour
1 tsp Baking powder
1 pinch Sea salt
20g Cocoa powder
100g Pecan nuts, broken pieces

method

1. Line a 30x20cm roasting pan with buttered greaseproof paper.
2. Melt the chocolate with the coffee 5 minutes/50°C/Speed 2 until smooth, pausing to scrape down the sides of the TM bowl once or twice.
3. Add remaining ingredients except the pecans and mix 30 seconds/Speed 5.
4. Add pecans and stir in 15 seconds/Speed 3/Reverse Blade Direction then transfer to prepared tin and use a pallet knife to spread out evenly.
5. Bake at 180°C for 20-25 minutes — they should still be a little soft in the middle when you take them out of the oven.
6. Cool in the pan and when cold, cut into small squares to serve.

NOTE:

If you wish to make a nut-free version, omit the nuts or replace them with white, milk and/or dark chocolate callets to create a 'mega chocolate' brownie or replace the nuts with raisins.

SHORTBREAD
CHOCOLATE BISCUITS

MAKES 30 TO 40 BISCUITS

ingredients

SHORTBREAD:

340g Plain white flour
270g Butter, diced, soft
110g Icing sugar
1 pinch Sea salt
3 Free-range medium egg whites
1 tsp Real vanilla extract

**DARK CHOCOLATE SAUCE
OR SPREAD:**

200g Double cream
250g Dark chocolate, small pieces
   or callets
25g Unsalted butter

TO FINISH:

Dark chocolate spread
Melted tempered chocolate of choice
Chopped nuts such as hazelnuts,
   pistachios or almonds

method

1. Mix flour, butter, sugar and salt 10 seconds/Speed 6.
2. Add egg whites and vanilla; mix 1 minute/Dough Setting – this makes a soft dough.
3. Use a star nozzle and pipe a variety of shapes in pairs onto silicone mats, decorating some with half glacé cherries, some with bake-stable chocolate drops, and leaving some plain.
4. Bake at 180°C for 8-10 minutes until pale gold and firm, remove from the oven and allow to cool.

5. To make the spread, pour the chocolate sauce into a suitable container or glass jar and let it set in the fridge for a couple of hours before using to fill these biscuits.

TO FINISH THE BISCUITS:

1. With a piping bag fitted with a star nozzle, pipe a layer of the chocolate spread onto the underside of one biscuit, place another on top; repeat to make more pairs, and allow to set.
2. When set, dip one end of each biscuit pair in melted tempered chocolate and sprinkle some chopped nuts on top.
3. Leave to set then store in an air-tight container.

DIRK'S VARIATIONS ON THE CHOCOLATE SAUCE/SPREAD:

1. Add some grated orange zest and some orange liqueur to the dark chocolate sauce and pour over a good vanilla ice cream.
2. Add some crushed chillies for a spicy chocolate sauce or spread.
3. Whisk some dark rum into the dark chocolate sauce, allow to set in the fridge for a couple of hours, then with a melon baller, scoop some of the spread and roll the little balls through dark cocoa powder to serve as rum truffles.

DARK CHOCOLATE SAUCE/SPREAD:

1. Heat the cream 4 minutes/80°C/Speed 2.
2. Add the chocolate and stir at Speed 2 until completely smooth, pausing to scrape down the sides of the TM bowl once or twice.
3. Add the butter and mix at Speed 2 until melted and smooth.
4. Serve straight away in a little jug as a hot sauce, or store in the fridge until needed and re-heat to 50°C at serving time.

"CHOCOLATE DOESN'T MAKE THE WORLD GO AROUND ... BUT IT CERTAINLY MAKES THE RIDE WORTHWHILE!"

ANON

LENZ BURGERLI

MAKES 60 PETITS FOURS OR 25 LONG BARS

ingredients

75g Flaked almonds
2 Tbsp Icing sugar
200g 33% milk chocolate, e.g.
    Callebaut 823 NV, small pieces or
    callets
100g Praline paste – see recipe p231
50g Candied orange peel,
    finely chopped
Milk chocolate, melted and
    tempered, for spreading
250g Gianduja, optional –
    see recipe p229

method

1. Spread the almonds on to a silicone mat, dust well with icing sugar and roast until golden in a preheated oven at 180ºC, watching carefully and mixing through from time to time, then leave to cool.

2. Heat the chocolate 2 minutes/50°C/Speed 2 – there should be a few unmelted callets up the sides of the TM bowl.

3. Scrape down, add the praline paste, cooled almonds and orange peel then stir 1 minute/Speed 3/Reverse Blade Direction.

4. Place an 8 or 10mm high frame 20x30cm onto a plastic sheet, pour in the mix and spread out level.

5. When set, thinly spread some melted milk chocolate on it, turn over onto another plastic sheet, then cover the (new) top with a thin layer of chocolate and mark to show the top, or cover with a layer of gianduja instead.

6. Cut into 60 little squares for petit fours, or into 25 long bars.

ROCKY ROAD

MAKES 18 PIECES 10CM X 3CM

ingredients

BASE:

350g Digestive biscuits, broken
230g Callebaut 823 NV, 33% milk
  chocolate, small pieces or callets
100g Unsalted butter, cold, diced

TOPPING:

100g Unsalted butter, cold, diced
250g Callebaut 823 NV, 33% milk
  chocolate, small pieces
  or callets
100g Walnuts, chopped
100g Glacé or dried cherries
200g Mini marshmallows

method

BASE:

1. Crush the digestive biscuits 20 seconds/Speed 4 until crumbs. Tip out and set aside.
2. Melt the chocolate and butter 2½ minutes/50°C/Speed 2 – at this point, half to three quarters of the chocolate should be melted.
3. Scrape down the sides of the TM bowl and stir 4 minutes/Speed 3 without heat until all the chocolate is melted.
4. Add the digestive crumbs and stir 20 seconds/Speed 3 or until well mixed.
5. Press into a 30x22cm frame or cake tin and chill in the fridge until set.

TOPPING:

1. Melt the butter and chocolate 2½ minutes/50°C/Speed 2 – at this point, half to three quarters of the chocolate should be melted.
2. Scrape down the sides of the TM bowl and stir 4 minutes/Speed 3 without heat or until all the chocolate is melted.
3. Add the chopped nuts, cherries and marshmallows and stir with the TM spatula until all are coated well.
4. Cover the base and leave to set for about 3-4 hours before cutting.
5. Keeps well in the fridge.

JANIE'S TIP:

If you prefer a less sweet version, make this recipe with dark chocolate instead of milk, and dried cherries instead of glacé cherries.

SPICY HOT CHOCOLATE

SERVES 1, EASILY MULTIPLIED

ingredients

SPICE MIX:

1 tsp Chilli flakes
2 Cinnamon sticks
2 tsp Cloves
1½ tsp Black peppercorns
1 whole Nutmeg
2 Star anise

FOR 1 DRINK:

50g Dark chocolate
250g Full-fat milk
½ to 1 tsp Spice mix (above), to taste
Whipped cream or marshmallows,
    to serve

method

1. Grind the spice mix 30 seconds/Speed 10. Transfer to a small glass jar with a lid – it keeps well in a dark cupboard.
2. Grate the chocolate 10 seconds/Speed 6.
3. Scrape down the sides of the TM bowl, add the milk and heat 4 minutes/80°C/Speed 3 (heat longer for more portions).

4. Froth 20 seconds/Speed 6.
5. Shake the spice mix into a tall latte glass. Pour the hot chocolate onto the spice mix and stir.
6. Decorate with whipped cream or marshmallows and serve, sweetening to taste if desired.

CHOCOLATE MACAROONS
WITH GOLD LEAF

MAKES 15-20 MACAROONS

ingredients

PASTRY CREAM:

60g Caster sugar
2 Free-range medium egg yolks
15g Cocoa powder
10g Custard powder
250g Whipping cream
½ Vanilla pod and seeds

MACAROONS:

100g Free-range egg whites
25g Caster sugar
120g Ground almonds
210g Icing sugar
20g Cocoa powder
Gold leaf, to decorate

method

PASTRY CREAM:

1. Cook all pastry cream ingredients 5 minutes/90°C/Speed 4.
2. Pour into a bowl and cool about 30 minutes, then transfer to a piping bag (can be chilled at this point).

MACAROONS:

1. Preheat the oven to 130°C without fan.
2. Insert the Butterfly Whisk into a clean grease-free TM bowl, add the egg whites and caster sugar and whisk 5 minutes/Speed 3 until stiff and glossy. Transfer to a large bowl.
3. In a clean dry TM bowl, sieve the ground almonds, icing sugar and cocoa powder by Turbo pulsing briefly a few times, then fold gently into the meringue.
4. Using two baking trays, place one on top of the other, then place a sheet of silicone paper on top.
5. Pour the mix into a piping bag with a 1cm nozzle and pipe small round macaroons, leaving about 1cm gap between each one.
6. Place a small piece of gold leaf on top of each macaroon, leave for about 30 minutes to form a slight crust, then bake for 15-20 minutes.
7. Remove from oven and remove the macaroons (still on the silicone sheet) from the baking tray – set aside to cool. Use a clean palette knife to lift one from the silicone sheet – if they are baked enough, it will come off quite easily. If it sticks, return the macaroons to the oven and bake a little longer. With macaroons, you are aiming for the perfect combination of dry outside and soft chewy inside.

ASSEMBLY:

1. When cooled pipe a little pastry cream onto one of the macaroons and sandwich together with another; repeat until all the macaroons have been paired. Chill in the fridge after adding the pastry cream - they taste even better the next day.

217

CHOCOLATE FRUIT SCONES

CHOCOLATE FRUIT SCONES

MAKES ABOUT 30 SCONES

ingredients

600g Plain white flour
1 pinch Sea salt
120g Caster sugar
3 tsp Baking powder
200g Very cold butter, cubed
200g Mixed dried fruit of choice
     (e.g. sultanas, cherries, raisins,
     citrus peel)
100g Dark bake-stable chocolate
     chunks or callets
370g Buttermilk
1 Egg, beaten (egg wash) to brush
     the scones

TO SERVE:
Butter
Clotted cream
Raspberry jam – see excellent
TM recipe in *'Demonstrator Delights'*

method

1. Mix dry ingredients and butter together 10 seconds/Speed 6 until you have a sandy texture.
2. Add the fruit, chocolate and buttermilk. Knead 20 seconds/Dough Setting.
3. Scrape down the sides of the TM bowl and knead again 10 seconds/Dough Setting.
4. Flatten the dough on a lightly floured surface to about 3cm thick and cut out scones.
5. Place on a silicone baking sheet and brush with egg wash.
6. Bake for about 25 minutes at 170°C.

TO SERVE:

1. Serve with butter, clotted cream and raspberry jam.

JANIE'S TIP:

Don't twist your scone cutter, or saw back and forth with your knife, just push straight down and lift straight up – a twisting or sawing motion could stop the scones from rising evenly.

COLD HOT CHILLI CHOCOLATE DRINK

MAKES 8 SHOT GLASSES

ingredients

250g Full-fat milk
½ Vanilla pod, split
1 Cinnamon stick 7-10cm long
1 Small red chilli, split with seeds removed
60g 54% dark chocolate, e.g. Callebaut 811 NV, small pieces or callets

method

1. Heat the milk, split vanilla pod, cinnamon stick and chilli 10 minutes/60°C/Speed 2.
2. Avoiding the TM blades, add the chocolate and stir at Speed 2 until melted.
3. Leave to infuse all the ingredients for approximately 10 minutes.
4. Pass through a sieve to remove the spices then cool and refrigerate.
5. When you are ready to serve, whisk at Speed 10 to create some foam and serve as is in shot glasses, or pour over crushed ice into espresso cups.

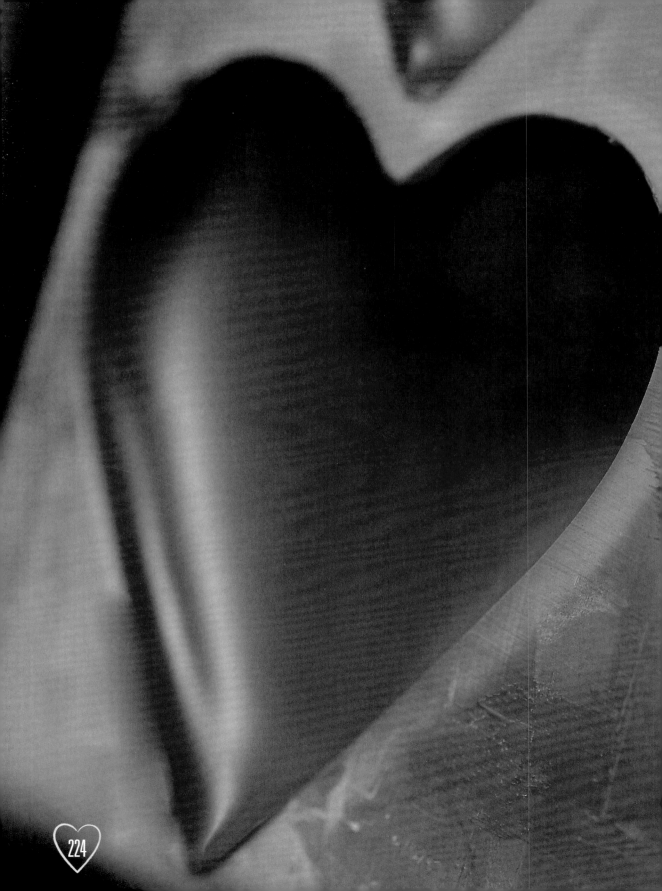

"FORGET LOVE ...
I'D RATHER FALL IN CHOCOLATE!"

225

FEUILLETINE

Feuilletine is used to add textural contrast to otherwise creamy sweets. You can fold it into a mousse, stir into a ganache, or try it sprinkled onto buttercream icing between layers of cake. It can be bought ready-made but making it yourself in your Thermomix means you can vary the size and thickness of the flakes, and you know that it's fresh and contains only natural ingredients.

ingredients

130g Unsalted butter, diced, soft
110g Brown sugar
3 tsp Baking powder
170g Molasses
370g Plain flour
55g Milk
1 Free-range large egg
Optional – orange zest, spice/s

method

1. Preheat oven to 180°C and prepare two large baking sheets each covered with a silicone mat.
2. Mix all the ingredients 1 minute/Speed 10, pausing once to scrape down the sides of the TM bowl with the spatula.
3. Put a small amount of the batter on each silicone mat then spread out very thinly using a palette knife or spatula. You want it as thin as possible, almost translucent.
4. Bake in the preheated oven for 8 minutes or until baked. Cool completely before crumbling into flakes (it should be crisp, so return any softer bits to the oven to dry out a little more).
5. Continue spreading and baking until you use up all the batter. The batter will keep in the fridge for a couple of days if you don't want to bake it all in one go.
6. Store in an airtight container – it should keep well for up to 6 weeks.

JANIE'S TIP:

If you don't have a silicone mat, you can use parchment paper but it's not quite the same. The batter is difficult to spread thinly enough over parchment, which tends to bunch up and wrinkle. Also once baked the feuilletine won't release cleanly from the parchment and the result is a few good flakes and a lot of powdery crumbs.

Feuilletine mix in TM bowl

Feuilletine on mat, ready to bake

Feuilletine flakes

Feuilletine stirred into praline paste, as used in Royale recipe p70

FRUIT PUREES

ingredients

500g ripe fruit, prepared as below
50g granulated sugar – optional
Lemon juice, freshly squeezed,
    to taste

method

1. Prepare fruit.
2. Cook if required with or without sugar (see notes below).
3. Blend at Speed 10 until smooth.
4. Taste and adjust flavour with lemon juice and/or more sugar if needed.

- For apricots, mangoes, apples, pears, peaches, nectarines, remove cores/pips/stones and peel mangoes/pears before puréeing.
- For melon, peel, remove seeds then blend.
- For rhubarb, remove leaves (they're poisonous), cut in 2 cm chunks, add sugar, cook 10 minutes/100°C/Speed 1, then blend.
- For raspberries, blueberries, blackberries, strawberries, elderberries, blend first then press through a fine sieve to remove the seeds.
- For fruit that has pips that are difficult to remove (e.g. small plums, greengages, damsons, gooseberries), mix and cook 500 g whole fruit 10-15 minutes/100°C/Speed 2/Reverse Blade Direction until the flesh is separated from the pips, then pour into the internal steaming basket or a sieve set over a bowl or a second TM bowl, press fruit through, discard pips, then blend.
- For pineapple, remove skin and core, cut fruit into 2cm chunks then blend.

For some of the more sour fruits, you may need to use a little more than 50g sugar – although for best flavour, the fresh or cooked purée should be slightly tart – hence you might like to add tartness to a very sweet fruit purée by adding a squeeze of fresh lemon juice.

JANIE'S TIP:

If I have lots of fruit, I like to make large batches of fruit purée 500g to 1kg at a time, as any extra can be frozen and used for a multitude of recipes throughout the year. I freeze fruit purées in ice cube trays then pop the frozen cubes into a freezer container so I can take out exactly the amount needed and defrost it quickly.

GIANDUJA

Gianduja keeps well in a sterilised jar in a cool place. Makes 250g. Easily doubled, tripled or quadrupled.

ingredients

170g milk chocolate, small pieces or callets
80g praline paste – see recipe p231

method

1. Melt the chocolate 4 minutes/37°C/Speed 3, pausing to scrape down the sides of the TM bowl twice.
2. Scrape down again, then stir 3 minutes/Speed 3 without heat until completely melted and smooth.
3. Add the praline paste and stir at Speed 3 to 4/Reverse Blade Direction until well mixed.

JANIE'S TIPS:

To make other quantities, basically you are using 70% milk chocolate by weight and 30% praline paste by weight to give you the total weight you want to make. It will take longer to melt larger quantities of chocolate of course. For a triple or quadruple quantity, melt the chocolate at 50°C instead of 37°C.

1. For 500g Gianduja, melt 350g milk chocolate and add 150g praline paste.
2. For 1kg, melt 700g milk chocolate and add 300g praline paste.

MARZIPAN

Home-made marzipan is easy to handle and much more delicious than commercial varieties. Can be wrapped tightly with greaseproof paper or cling film and then stored airtight in a bag or box in the fridge. Makes about 500g.

ingredients

240g granulated sugar, divided 100g and 140g
220g blanched almonds
2 free-range medium egg yolks, plus 1 extra if needed
1 Tbsp lemon juice
1 Tbsp orange flower water or rose water
¼ tsp real vanilla extract (not flavouring)
1 tsp almond extract, or more to taste (not flavouring)

method

1. Weigh 100g of the granulated sugar into the TM bowl, grind to **caster sugar** 5 seconds/Speed 10. Tip out and set aside.
2. Weigh remaining 140g granulated sugar into the TM bowl, grind to **icing sugar** 1 minute/Speed 10. Set aside in a wide flat bowl or on a plate.
3. Weigh the blanched almonds (they must be dry) into the TM bowl and grind until fine 10 seconds/Speed 10.
4. Add the caster sugar and most of the icing sugar (save 2 Tbsp for Step 6). Mix 10 seconds/Speed 3.
5. Add egg yolks and flavourings. Knead 1 minute/Dough Setting until a rough paste is formed – add the other egg yolk if it still looks like crumbs, then knead again 30 seconds/Dough Setting.
6. Taste and add more almond extract if desired – knead 30 seconds/Dough Setting if you've added more. Turn out of the TM bowl and use the remaining icing sugar to roll out the marzipan if needed.

PRALINE PASTE

Very easy to make when you have a Thermomix. Makes 1 kg. Stores well in a jar in the fridge for up to 1 month.

ingredients

600g mixed nuts – pistachios, cashews, pecans, macadamia, almonds, hazelnuts
400g caster sugar
100g water

method

1. In a deep heavy-bottomed sauté pan, bring sugar and water to a boil and continue to boil without stirring until temperature reaches 116°C on a temperature probe.
2. Add nuts and stir until all are coated. The sugar will soon crystalise, but will re-melt as you continue.
3. Keep on cooking and stirring for another 20 minutes or so until it caramelises (turns golden coloured) but does not burn. Immediately pour out onto a greased tray or silicone mat and leave to cool completely.
4. Break any large pieces into 5-7 cm size then grind the whole batch in your Thermomix at Speed 10 until you hear it flicking up onto the sides of the TM bowl.
5. Scrape down the bowl with the spatula and continue blending at Speed 5 until you have a nice creamy paste.

TIP:

If you want to use only one type of nut, feel free – a classic praline paste would contain only hazelnuts.

Sugar crystalising

Finished praline before grinding to paste

OVEN TEMPERATURES

Celsius*	Fahrenheit **	Gas	Description
110°C	225°F	Gas Mark 1/4	Cool
120°C	250°F	Gas Mark 1/2	Cool
130°C	275°F	Gas Mark 1	Very low
150°C	300°F	Gas Mark 2	Very low
160°C	325°F	Gas Mark 3	Low
180°C	350°F	Gas Mark 4	Moderate
190°C	375°F	Gas Mark 5	Moderate, Hot
200°C	400°F	Gas Mark 6	Hot
220°C	425°F	Gas Mark 7	Hot
230°C	450°F	Gas Mark 8	Very hot
240°C	475°F	Gas Mark 9	Very hot

* For fan assisted ovens, reduce Centigrade temperatures by 10-20°C as per manufacturer's instructions

** For fan assisted ovens, reduce Fahrenheit temperatures by 25-50°F as per manufacturer's instructions

ACETATE
Sheets used for lining moulds and containers for a smooth finish.

AERATE
The process of allowing air to combine into ingredients to make then lighter and/or create more volume.

CALLETS
Chocolate callets are bits of chocolate, similar to chocolate chips in size, but without the traditional shape of a chocolate chip.

COCOA BLOCK
After roasting, cocoa beans are ground finely into a cocoa mass or paste. The mass is then melted and becomes liquor. The liquor is cooled and moulded into blocks known as cocoa block or unsweetened baking chocolate or bitter chocolate.

CONCERTINA
To fold, crush or push together.

COULIS
A thick sauce made of puréed fruit – see recipe p228.

COUVERTURE
Chocolate that is a very high quality containing extra cocoa butter (32-39%).

DARIOLE MOULD
A cylindrical, slightly tapered mould for both cooking and serving individual desserts.

FEUILLETINE
A rough, crunchy textured biscuit.

FONDANT
1. A powdered form of icing sugar, but 100 times finer grind.
2. A smooth creamy mixture, often used as an accompaniment, filling or cake covering.

FRANGELICO
A hazelnut liqueur from Northern Italy.

FRIAND
A small French cake, often mistaken for a pastry.

GANACHE
A glaze, icing or filling made from chocolate and cream.

GENOISE
A very light Italian sponge cake closely associated with Italian and French cooking, forming the basic building block of much French pâtisserie.

GLAZE
A coating of glossy, often sweet, mixture applied to food.

GRIOTTINE CHERRIES
Cherries macerated in eau de vie or kirsch.

INFUSE
To flavour or scent a liquid by steeping ingredients in it.

MERINGUE
A mixture of stiffly beaten egg whites and sugar, used as the basis for soufflés, sponges, pie and tart coverings or baked in small portions or large as a cake or a dessert.

MILLEFEUILLE
A pastry of French origin traditionally made up of 3 layers of puff pastry alternated with crème pâtissière.

MYCRYO®
Mycryo® is pure cocoa butter in dry, powder form, ideal for baking.

PALETTE KNIFE
A knife with a round-ended flexible blade used for scraping out a mixture from a bowl or spreading icing.

PARCHMENT PAPER
A cellulose based paper used in baking as a disposable non-stick surface.

PARFAIT
A frozen creamy dessert often served in slices or quenelles.

PRALINE
A confection made of nut kernels, especially almonds or pecans, stirred in boiling sugar syrup until crisp and brown.

PUREE
1. To blend or strain food until a thick consistency; 'blend until a purée'.
2. Food that has been blended or strained.

RAMEKIN
A small individual circular, porcelain glass or earthenware oven-proof dish.

ROSETTE
A rose-like shape.

ROULADE
A sponge cake or cake baked in a flat pan then rolled around a filling.

ROYAL ICING
A hard, white icing made from softly beaten egg whites, icing sugar and sometimes lemon juice. Sets to a smooth, matte finish.

SABLE PASTRY
A sweet pastry dough used for lining tarts.

SILPAT
A popular silicone mat used in baking to provide a non-stick surface without fat.

SNOBINETTE
A small hand dipped chocolate cup made to hold fondants, icings and creams.

SOUFFLE
A light, fluffy baked dish made with egg yolks and beaten egg whites.

SPRING FORM MOULD
A type of bakeware that keeps the food in shape and features sides that can be removed from the base.

TEMPER
To bring chocolate to the desired consistency, texture or temperature.

TOFFOC
Toffee vodka from Wales.

VERMICELLI
Name given in the UK to small chocolate sprinkles.

237

NOTES

NOTES